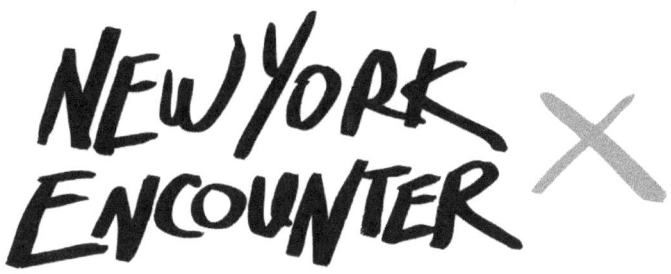

NEW YORK ENCOUNTER

"Here Begins a New Life"

Dante Alighieri

This book contains transcripts, not reviewed by the authors, of talks given at the New York Encounter 2025

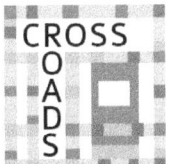

Crossroads Cultural Center

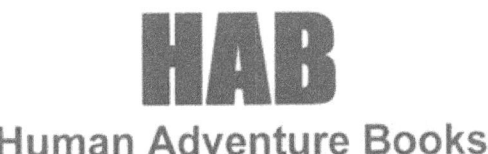

HAB

Human Adventure Books

Transcription & Layout
Deep River Media, LLC

Publisher
Human Adventure Books

Contents

"Here Begins a New Life"

Dante Alighieri

New York Encounter 2025

We "modern" men and women have a difficult relationship with the past. We are told that it was rife with injustice and oppression, and that tradition is a straitjacket restraining our freedom. We tend to think that everything old is, by default, obsolete. We like reinventing, or "rebranding," our persona, leaving behind the history that shaped it. In the name of a better future, we risk losing memory of the past.

We are paying a price for this loss. In school, education is increasingly about securing a well-paid job, rather than awakening curiosity and handing down a common heritage. At work, different generations no longer seem to share the same ideals and have a hard time communicating. In social life, we stick with our online tribe or we "bowl alone." Ignorance of history opens the door to manipulation by the powerful. Above all, the lack of roots generates a feeling of precariousness. It fills the present with anxiety and empties the future of its promise. Is there hope?

Recalling his first meeting with Beatrice, who, for the rest of his life, would embody beauty itself, Dante Alighieri writes:

> *In that part of the book of my memory, before which little can be read, there is a heading that says: 'Here begins a new life.'*

The encounter with a great love gives us a glimpse of a mysterious presence — the ultimate Beauty and Love — whom we always expected but never met. The awareness of this presence, its memory, can heal our relationship with the past and give reasons to hope and to build. Within this experience, "whatever you remember is a fragment of being that rises from the sepulcher, and the different fragments, coming together, rearrange themselves into a design that is no longer just a promise, but a promise that is already being fulfilled" (Fr. Luigi Giussani). All that is needed is our attention.

New York Encounter 2025

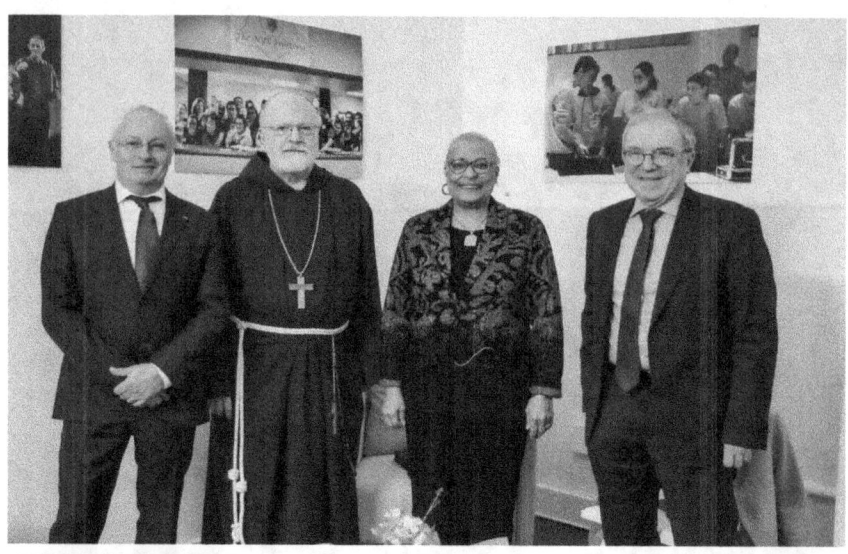

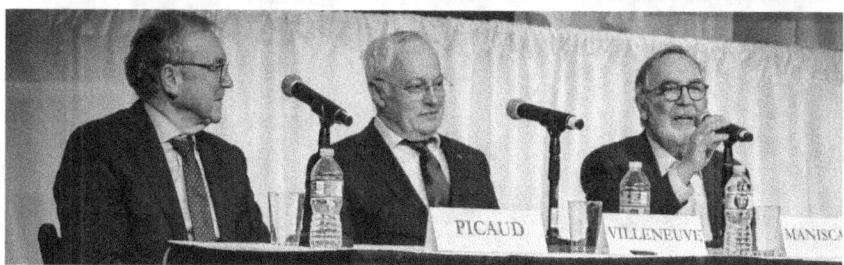

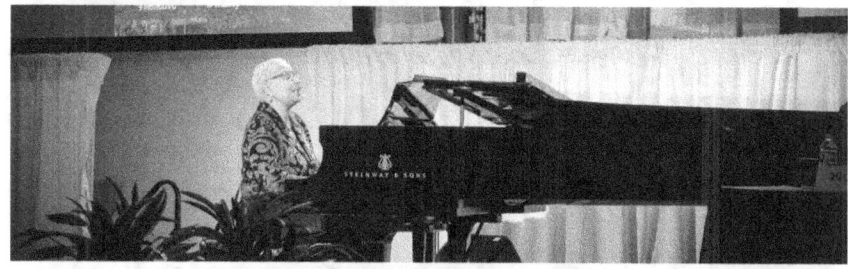

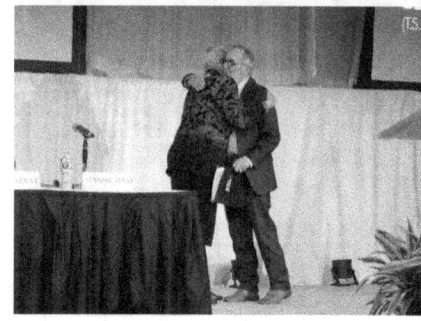

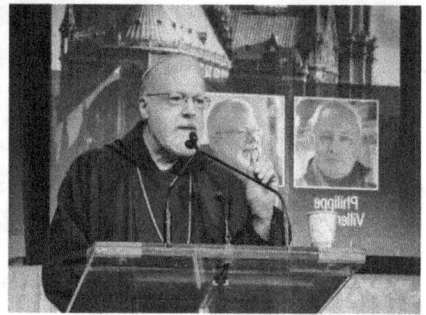

"Forever building, and always decaying, and always being restored." (T.S. Eliot)

*The Encounter opens with a presentation by **Philippe Villeneuve**, Chief Architect of the Reconstruction of the Cathedral of Notre Dame in Paris, and introduced by **Cardinal Seán O'Malley**, Archbishop Emeritus of Boston.*

Introduction

"What has to happen, in order for the new encounter to be the 'new encounter' is to become again what we were. What were we? Nothing! Therefore, we must become again what we were, illuminated by a light that no one could build, could build for himself, on his own. The new beginning is the object of an entreaty, of a begging."

— Fr. Luigi Giussani

✠

Riro Maniscalco: Good evening, everybody, and welcome to New York Encounter 2025. Thank you to Vaneese Thomas for the gift of her presence and performance. It's like an invitation and encouragement to live this weekend with our eyes open, our hearts and our minds open, so that the encounter with the great love may actually happen, and that we may be vigilant and open to acknowledge it and to follow the path it indicates. We take a first step onto the battlefield with a longtime friend of ours, Cardinal Seán O'Malley, who will share with us his reflections and his thoughts about the theme. So I invite Cardinal O'Malley to come here to the podium.

Cardinal Seán O'Malley: Good evening, everyone. It's a great joy to be back at the New York Encounter, which is such an extraordinary event. For so many years I've been coming here, and each time it's an enriching experience.

Recently, someone asked me, What are your pronouns? Now, when you ask someone 80 years old what their pronouns are, it's pretty disarming. But I decided that my pronouns are *thou/thine*. And please remember that *thine* is always used before a vowel. [*audience laughter*]

When I was a young priest working at the Spanish Catholic Center in Washington, there was a terrible earthquake in Guatemala. It was in 1976 and the quake was 7.5 on the Richter scale. Thousands of people died. I was contacted by an NGO in Washington because they were sending someone down to help out, and they wanted me to help find a very remote area where people probably would not be getting any help from anyone else. And I had a friend in those days, Adolfo Menendez, who did a lot of photography for *National Geographic* and would travel way out into the most rural areas, and was on very good terms with a number of the indigenous tribes out there. He took this man from the NGO there, who met with the chief and the leadership of this tribe, and explained that he was there to underwrite any one project that they could identify as their most important need, whether it was a clinic or a school or potable water, whatever. And the chieftain said, Well, we have to bring the community together to make this decision. And so they had their meeting. Afterwards, the chieftain came back and said, We decided that our greatest need is to repair our church, which was damaged by the earthquake.

Seeing the great need and the poverty of the people, the man from the NGO was completely shocked. It never would have occurred to him that they would identify that as their most important need the repairing of their church. Pope Francis in *Evangelii Gaudium* says how quick we are to provide material aid to people, and how slow we are and how neglectful we are about their spiritual needs.

Eight-hundred years ago, a bishop and a poor friar were both working on churches. The bishop was working on a church in Paris that eventually became Notre Dame, a church that could hold 9000 people. The friar was

St Francis, who was building a different church in honor of Our Lady, the portiuncula, that held about 25 people. In these last 800 years, how many millions of people have passed through these churches, which have been the gate of heaven for many believers, addressing the longing of the human heart for meaning, for beauty, for community, and for all that's tied up in our hunger for God? That tiny church of St Francis was rebuilt at God's request: *Rebuild my Church.* Today, we're getting the same marching orders. *Rebuild God's Church.* That's the way we will bring new life into our world.

Rebuilding the portiuncula and the Cathedral of Notre Dame have had a huge impact on the world. The reopening of Notre Dame is truly a sign of hope, a sign of Jubilee, the reset button of our spiritual longings. I was reminding Philippe and the people who've come from Notre Dame that for over 200 years, the Capuchin friars ran the fire department in the city of Paris. I told him, if we were still running it, that fire would never have taken place.

A recent survey taken by Pew reveals that for the first time in our history, more Americans would prefer not to have children. Never have we had so many dying of suicide and drug overdoses. Our Holy Father has given us this new Jubilee Year so that more people will truly be able to say, *Here begins a new life.* We are a people of hope, and the New York Encounter always brings us together as pilgrims of hope. The first encyclical in the New Testament is the first epistle of St Peter, and in that document the first pope tells us to be ready to give an explanation for the reasons for our hope to all who ask. I hope that all of us will be both pilgrims of hope and witnesses of hope, as Pope Francis asks of us.

Growing up in a large Irish Catholic family, there were certain rituals that we observed every year, and one of them was of particular importance, and that's when my nana, my grandmother, would take us each year on August second to Rocky River Drive, because there were three Franciscan houses there. One was the Poor Clare monastery, then the Franciscan friars, Our Lady the Angels, and then the parish school that was run by the Sisters of St Joseph of the Third Order of St Francis. In those days, the Church offered a plenary indulgence each time the faithful entered a Franciscan chapel and offered prayers for the intentions of the Holy Father.

You could gain a plenary indulgence for every church visited that day, I remember the throngs of people circulating between those three churches, gaining the indulgences, leaving one church, going to the next. We were part of that column.

At one point we entered the chapel of the Poor Clares and my grandmother announced which relative we were getting out of purgatory. I was getting tired and bored, and I said, "Nana, we got that one out last year." She was unmoved by my protest and simply responded that one needs a lot of prayers. [*audience laughter*]

According to the ancient tradition, St Francis asked Pope Honorius III to grant an indulgence to all devout pilgrims who visited the chapel of Our Lady the Angels on August 2. Pope Francis, in his bull of convocation for the Jubilee of 2025, talks about St Francis's intervention to establish the portiuncula feast, the *Pardon of Assisi* as it's called in Italian. This was one of the historic events that inspired Pope Boniface to institute the custom of the Holy Year. The first Holy Year was in the year 1300, and in the last eight centuries years there have been 32 Holy Years convoked by the popes. The Church's Holy Year finds inspirations in St Francis's portiuncula indulgence, and in the Old Testament Jubilee. In the Old Testament, every seventh year was a Sabbath year, and a week of Sabbath years was 50 years. That was the Jubilee, and the Jubilee was a moment when they would experience an economic, cultural, environmental, and communal reset, when the people and the land would rest and all those who were in slavery would be set free. The cry of Jubilee could be, "Here begins a new life!" For Dante, that Life began when he saw the beauty of Beatrice. For us, the Jubilee should be a renewed encounter with God's mercy and love, an encounter with brothers and sisters who are fellow pilgrims on the journey of faith and hope.

Welcome to the New York Encounter in this Jubilee Year as pilgrims of hope, ever ready to discover the path that allows us to say with Dante, *Here begins a new life*. Welcome, and God bless you.

Riro Maniscalco: Thank you, Cardinal O'Malley. Building a dwelling place for people from all walks of life, and restoring a dwelling place for people from all walks of life, for all peoples—this is what brought us to invite

Philippe Villeneuve, chief architect of the reconstruction of the Cathedral of Notre Dame in Paris. So I invite Philippe Villeneuve on stage to join us and share with us his adventure with the reconstruction of the cathedral.

Philippe Villeneuve: Thank you very much. I'm going to try to speak in English, and I'm going to do it quickly, because I have to present to you five years of work, very special work: the reconstruction of Notre Dame.

Images appear on the screen behind him

You can recognize me in the photos, but all around you can also see many architects. There are one or two engineers, who were not very important for the reconstruction. [*audience laughter*] Because for eight centuries there were no engineers, just architects, so I try to do the same without engineers. [*audience laughter*]

In these three pictures, the most important is perhaps this one in the middle, because you can see a very important symbol of the cathedral: the statue of Notre Dame de Paris. You can see in front of this statue the stone and the wood, the burnt wood of the spire, and to the right, you can see the other piece of wood of the spire down on the nave. To the left, you can see the three holes in the vault. This enormous hole in the vault presented a problem for us. We had to ensure that the cathedral wall wouldn't collapse more after the fire, because indeed the vault could collapse. Perhaps the wall above the roses could collapse. Perhaps the sculptures could fall down above the walls of the nave. So it was very important to protect all of the cathedral. We placed umbrellas over the opening to protect the church below.

But there was much we didn't know. How sturdy was the vault? Perhaps it would fall down in five minutes, or perhaps in two weeks, or perhaps in one month. We didn't know, and we couldn't take a chance of people working beneath such an unstable structure. So we used robots, as you can see in the photos, and we had to pay attention so that no element of the cathedral structure moved. If the vaults were to fall down, then the flying buttresses would continue to push on the wall and make the wall fall down. That's why, as you can see in the picture, we built new scaffolding. I had to evacuate all the elements that were touched by the fire. The old scaffolding was completely burned and destroyed.

We had to build a very impressive scaffolding to rebuild the spire. This scaffolding began from the ground and had to go 100 meters high and weighed 600 tons. So it's very, very heavy. We knew that in the ground there were many sepulchers, and we discovered this wonderful piece [*motions to the photo on the screen*], which we hope will be displayed in a new museum of Notre Dame.

You know that the fire destroyed all the carpentry and the roof. The roof was made with lead, constitutes a pollution and was very dangerous for the workers. We had to use a vacuum, a very powerful vacuum. And after we put latex on the wall and on the vault, and as you can see in this photograph, we discovered traces of a decoration created for the baptism of Napoleon III's son. You can see the little details.

We then restored the vaults. The vaults had been damaged in just three areas, but all the rest of the vaults withstood the fire and the water. At Notre Dame, the vaults did the job their medieval architects intended.

Chapels around the church had been decorated with imagination by Viollet-le-Duc. It's like during one century in France, we didn't like Viollet-le-Duc, who suddenly was considered a bad architect. A fantasist with imagination but not very serious. That's why all the chapels of the nave had the same decorations that you can see here. After the fire, we restored these decorations, and you can see that it's wonderful. It's perhaps not medieval, but still, it's a neo-Gothic style invented by Viollet-le-Duc, and it's the beginning of the Art Nouveau. It was a new art, you know, in the beginning of the 20th century.

You can see this statue, which was moved four days before the fire. It's like Miss Liberty in New York, and it's not a joke. For the first centenary of American independence, France decided to offer a wonderful statue, Miss liberty. But Viollet-le-Duc died and the statue was not finished. An engineer was brought in, and finally you have at Notre Dame the first iteration of the Statue of Liberty in New York.

To rebuild this spire, it was not easy. Perhaps if this fire had happened five years earlier, or 20 or 30, then perhaps we wouldn't have rebuilt it in its original manner. Maybe in concrete or steel, I don't know. But I wanted to rebuild this spire properly because it's important and because the majority of people wanted to see again. It's their cathedral.

I show you here many pictures of the architect's building plans.

Images appear and progress on the screen behind him

It's the same technology as the Middle Ages. We used the same material as the original builders did because the church had never suffered destruction before. There had been little restorations here and there, but over eight centuries never a complete rebuilding. So why use other materials now? We considered it very important to pay attention to pollution and carbon. So when I cut down a tree, I planted another to replace it.

We put the decoration of the roof in lead, so you can in the photos many details, the same as created by Viollet-le-Duc. Here you can see the vault rebuilt, and you can see the rest of the vaults of the crossing with one of the four angels. We rebuilt this vault and recreated the four angels.

Here you can see other decorations of the inner chapels with their paintings. The paintings are a very important in Notre Dame. There was a congregation who, every year, offered to Notre Dame on the first of May a painting. So there was a very impressive collection. But after the Revolution, all the paintings were dispersed.

There are three miracles of this restoration. The first, as I show you, it's the protection of the statue of the Virgin you can see here. The second miracle was that in the church you have three very important statues. Louis XIII, upon the birth of his son, decided to put France under the protection of the Virgin. So he decided to make a new decoration in the church—three statues: Louis XIII, Louis IV, and, in the middle, the Virgin with the body of Jesus, just after the crucifixion. It's beautiful. And the third miracle is this rooster, because when the spire fell down in the fire, nobody saw the rooster. After the fire, I went on the north tower and I saw on a little green point that turn out to be the rooster of Notre Dame. It's a miracle because inside the rooster you had three precious relics: one of St Genevieve, another of St Denis, the protector of Paris, and a piece of Jesus' crown of thorns, which was the main relic preserved in this cathedral since the time of St Louis. I decided to draw a new rooster, one that looked like a rooster but also resembled fire, because this evokes the image of a Phoenix. But also because it symbolizes the Holy Spirit descending upon this cathedral. And inside, there are the three relics of the original rooster, as well as a manuscript that lists all the names of the companions who helped rebuild this cathedral. It was very important for me to add this, because I couldn't have done this work without these wonderful people.

Viollet-le-Duc placed a statue of himself in the basement of the church, at the base of the orginal spire, and it portrays him looking up at the spire. Four days before the fire, his statue was moved. At some point in the future, though, I'm going to put Viollet-le-Duc back in front of the spire. He will see that it's a new spire, and that there is another architect looking down at him from the spire.

Image of a small statue of Philippe Villeneuve looking down

"Hello there!" [*audience laughter*] Yes, it's funny, but symbolically it's very important to me, because my name is nowwhere on this cathedral, and there is no date. And of course, no one will recognize me in a century.It symbolizes all the companions, all the architects and engineers who helped rebuild this cathedral. It's just a little joke, and something of a tradition. Nobody understands all these these little symbols, and that's why this was a wonderful experience, rebuilding Notre Dame. I thank you and I apologize for my poor English.

Riro Maniscalco: A personal question. We know you restored in five years something that had taken a century to build. But at the personal level, your personal experience, I mean, you were entrusted with something extremely precious. Did you ever feel intimidated by the task?

Philippe Villeneuve: I am completely, as you can see, a little crazy. But no, more seriously, I have loved this cathedral since I was five years old. My grandfather gave me books about the cathedral, and other people in my family gave me other books on Notre Dame and its chapels. Later I saw this cathedral in person, and its architecture. So I fell in love with this cathedral. For me, it's very heavy to to understand that perhaps from my my birth to now I was meant to do this. I often say that I was like Joan of Arc, completely determined. I saw my cathedral burning. For me, it meant I had to go rebuild this cathedral. [*audience applause*]

Riro Maniscalco: Thank you, Mr. Villeneuve. Now it's getting late. We're all it's time to move to the next step. There's a lot to see. There's a lot to visit here at the New York Encounter. There's a food court. There are exhibits on the fifth floor. And we'll meet again here at 9:00 PM for a big concert, a piano concert in memory of Father Luigi Giussani. Thank you.

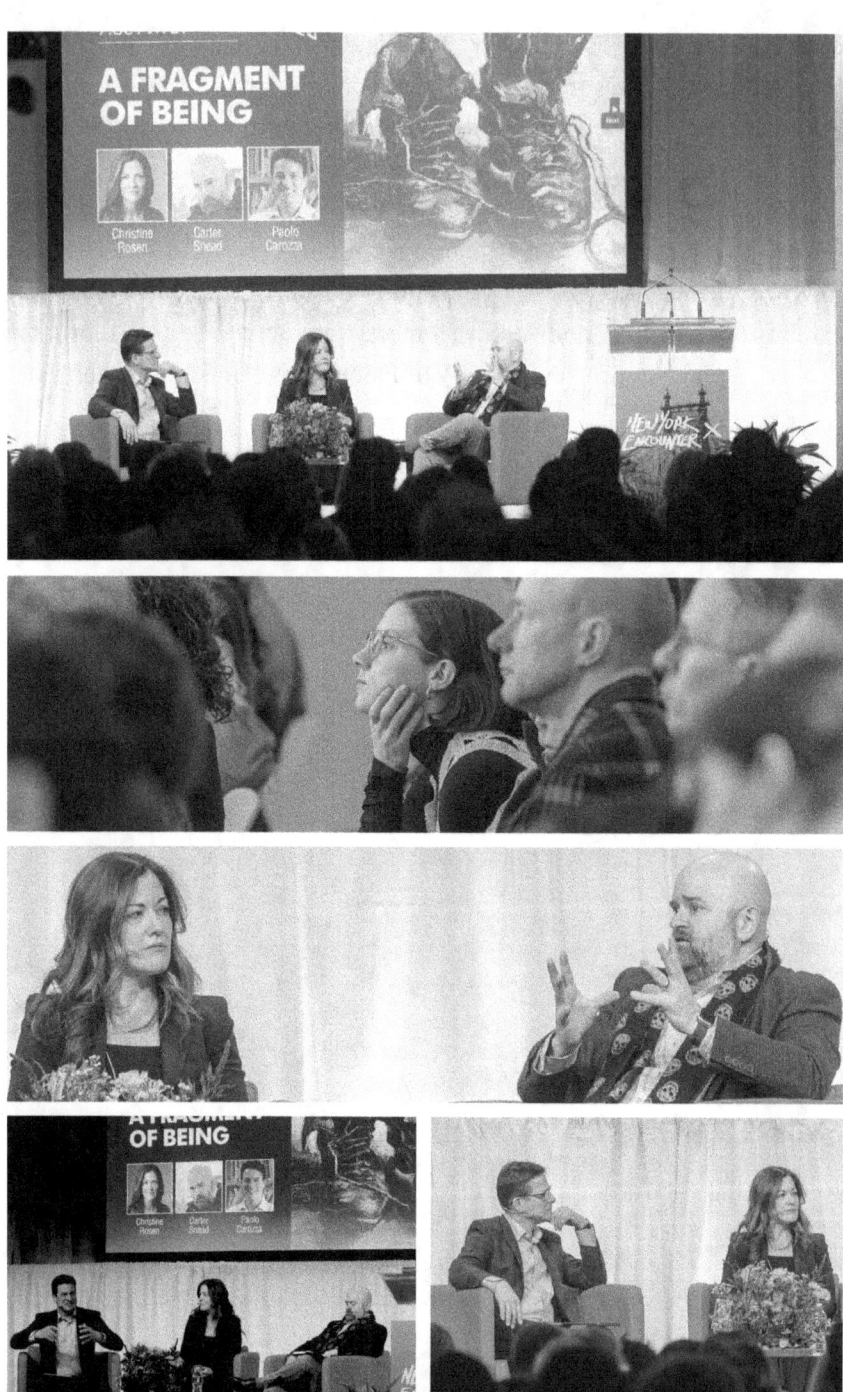

A Fragment of Being

*A discussion on the corporal dimension of human identity in an age of virtual reality, with **Christine Rosen**, Senior Fellow at the American Enterprise Institute, and **Carter Snead**, Professor of Law, University of Notre Dame. Moderated by **Paolo Carozza**, Professor of Law, University of Notre Dame.*

Introduction

A troubling cultural trend is a vision of humanity that invites us to obliterate the corporeal dimension of our being through the application of increasingly invasive and sophisticated technologies. The speakers have explored this issue and its negative repercussions and will dialogue on the need to rediscover the bodily component of our human identity amid growing virtual realities.

✠

Paolo Carozza: Welcome to the first session of the Saturday program of the New York Encounter. It's wonderful to see so many people here, including the volunteers who have made it possible for us to be together again this year. My name is Paolo Carrozza. I'm a professor of law at the University of Notre Dame, and I have the honor this morning of hosting two guests to help us talk about what we've entitled "A Fragment of Being." We'll focus on the memory of the human body and how important—yet often lost—it is in our current environment.

Let me introduce our wonderful guests. Christine Rosen, to my left, is a senior fellow at the American Enterprise Institute. She focuses on questions relating to American history, society, technology, culture, and feminism. Her background is as a historian, with a PhD from Emory University.

She's a prolific author of many books, but most relevant to our topic today is her recent work titled *The Extinction of Experience: Being Human in a Disembodied World.*

Our second guest, Carter Snead, my longtime friend from the University of Notre Dame Law School, is the Charles E. Rice Professor of Law there and a concurrent professor of political science. He's one of the world's leading experts on public bioethics. For 12 years, he was the director of Notre Dame's de Nicola Center for Ethics and Culture, which I think probably learned a few things from the New York Encounter and the Meeting in Rimini over the years. He is also the author of numerous articles and books, including his 2020 book, listed by *The Wall Street Journal* as one of the best books of the year in any subject, titled *What It Means to Be Human: The Case for the Body in Public Bioethics.*

Christine and Carter, I'm so happy to help organize this conversation with the two of you. In my work in the technology sector over the last few years, one of the most striking things I've noticed is an underlying, pervasive kind of dualism about the human person. This dualism, which seems to be at the root of so much in this sector, treats the human being as if it were just a disembodied mind. I'm eager to understand where this comes from, how it manifests in our culture, what some of its implications are, and lastly, what we can do about it—and how to respond to it.

Both of your books were so striking to me because, coming from very different perspectives and disciplines—academics, public policy, history, law—and even addressing different technologies, you nevertheless converge around this point about the essential need for remembering the body and embodiment.

So, let's start by trying to—pardon the pun—put some flesh on the problem. What are some specific, concrete examples or manifestations of the problem of disembodiment, or of forgetting the centrality of the human body in the world today, that you've written about and are worried about? Christine, why don't we start with you?

Christine Rosen: Sure. Thank you, Paolo, and thank you all for being here and to New York Encounter. I would say that the technological mindset that dominates our culture today sees both the human body and human nature and the human person as obstacles to be overcome, problems to be solved, whereas those of us who come from a background of the humanities or faith understand the human person to be embodied at all times. And so from my perspective, the risk that most poses a challenge to us on a daily basis is that the convenience that our technologies offer us—the ease and the efficiency which we love, whether we want to admit it or not—actually challenge us to think and ignore our bodily signals. We begin to prefer mediated communication to face-to-face communication. We begin to mistrust our own emotional responses to things unless they're reflected on a social media page and we get enough likes for them. So in that sense, we're habituating ourselves to a deeply disembodied way of seeking approval, of understanding the world we live in. And what that's led to, besides higher rates of anxiety and depression among those who most heavily mediate their experience, is a misunderstanding of what we owe each other as human beings, that we owe showing up for people, particularly who are sick or weak or need our help. And I think in very mundane ways, our daily experience has deteriorated because of this mindset, which grew, not with any sort of nefarious intent, but over time. You step on a subway platform and people are more rude, there seems to be more hostility and anger and impatience. So I think the great challenge ahead is becoming more familiar with what embodied human experience means in terms of our daily behavior as individuals, but more importantly as members of families and communities.

Paolo Carozza: Yeah, thank you. Carter, public bioethics is very different from just sort of a general cultural critique, but obviously one of the things that's most compelling about your book is the way that you interweave those things, right? That the public bioethical sphere is not divorced from the larger cultural presumptions and attitudes that we have. Where do you see this disembodiment manifesting itself concretely in our social life?

Carter Snead: I'd first like to join Christine in thanking everyone for having us here. It's a very special thing to be at the New York Encounter, especially with my dear friend Christine, who I haven't seen for 20 years. But it's amazing.

Christine Rosen: And we haven't aged a day.

Carter Snead: It's amazing, almost like we don't have bodies. [*audience laughter*]

So a lot of people who haven't thought much about law usually imagine law as separate and distinct from cultural norms or concepts of embodiment or personhood and so on, but in fact they're deeply intertwined because of what law is for. And this is a broad statement—to an extent, a presupposition about what a person is and what human flourishing is. Otherwise, the law is arbitrary or capricious or worse. And so in the way that Christine was saying, we negotiate our daily lives thinking about who we are and what our flourishing is, and we have these mediated experiences. The law is built on presuppositions. And if the law imagines a person to be merely a disembodied will or an atomized individual will whose highest flourishing is simply to discover the authentic, original truths inside of yourself and to express them and to project a life plan and to follow that life plan, and that is, reductively, what we are, then the law is going to look a lot different than if we imagine human beings as dynamic psychophysical unities of body and mind; that we don't *have* bodies but *are* bodies, and are, as a result, fragile and dependent and vulnerable. And therefore we stand in a particular kind of relationship to one another, one of reciprocal dependence. And what our flourishing requires that the law has to encode and embed, or at least make space for private ordering to take care of what we need.

For our flourishing is not simply the freedom of the unencumbered will to do what we want, but rather what McIntyre calls networks of uncalculated giving and graceful receiving, made up of people who are willing to make the good of others their own good without counting the cost. That's what human beings need to flourish precisely because we are bodies, to put it more succinctly, because we are living and dying bodies. We are made for love and friendship, and you can know that by thinking about embodied experience. And if you only think of yourself as a disembodied will, not only do you imagine there are no clues to how you should live in nature itself, in terms of the configuration of your own body or relationships of the natural world, everything is constructed by you according to your own interior truth. If that's how you see the world, then you can't make sense of fragility or vulnerability. And as Christine said, you can't even see the vulnerable others who have claims on you that aren't a function of contract or consent or some kind of prior agreement. There are people who have claims on us that we don't choose. There are unearned privileges that we have and unchosen obligations that we have. And the only way you can see that in a kind of incarnational way is to understand that we stand in relationships to each other precisely because of our vulnerability, which is a function of our embodiment and flourishing. It looks an awful lot different viewed through that lens than it does to the disembodied will.

Paolo Carozza: That's a great way to start. You mentioned along the way, Carter, you know, living, dying, love, friendship. I mean, any one of those I'd love to hone in on. I'm tempted to talk about AI and romantic relationships in light of the recent statistics of studies that show as many as 40% of adults in the United States have engaged in some form of interaction with a bot intended to simulate a romantic relationship, which is pretty frightening, but I'm gonna set that temptation aside, having just noted that—

Carter Snead: What does that mean to the crowd in the room?

Paolo Carozza: Look to your left. Look to your right. Those are bodies, not bots. I'm gonna focus instead, though, on the living and dying part, right? Let's hone in on an example where it really comes to roots, these things in concrete ways, culturally as well as politically and legally. What about age and dying? Right? I mean, how do you see this disembodiment and this forgetting of this fragment of our being, which is the body playing out in things like, you know, the resistance against aging and how we treat those who are dying?

Christine Rosen: Well, I'll give you two brief stories to illustrate the habits of mind we've formed as human beings because of our technologies. And use both of these as an example of why we have to now actively choose the human interaction because the default is no longer human. So telepresence robots that are used in hospitals are sort of robots on wheels, and you slap an iPad on the top of it, and you have a real human person through the screen, a doctor consultant. These can be very useful in rural areas and areas that aren't close to hospitals. But one was used to tell a man that he had terminal cancer, and that's wrong. There is no argument for efficiency or convenience that should lead us to believe that a telepresence robot should ever deliver that news to a human being. Look to care homes, particularly in aging countries such as Japan, where the young don't feel they have time to spend with their elderly relatives. They have devised robots that look like pet seals or other animals, and they place them on the laps of the older residents, and they can pet the animal and they feel better. And the argument that's always made for these substitutes for human contact are, well, it's better than nothing. And I think our world now requires each and every one of us to say, No, it's not. That's not good enough. And so when we think about the things we're choosing to mediate our obligations, particularly for care for the most vulnerable populations, the elderly, the people who are ill and children, because these are the populations that our technologists most like to experiment upon, because they are the weaker, they don't have a voice in a lot of these cultural discussions. I would say those examples, and those are just two, there are many, many more, where we as a culture, again, without thinking through the implications, the ethical choices we're making here are just assuming that the new thing is the better thing, and in many of these cases, it simply isn't.

Carter Snead: Listening to you say that I remember there was a picture during COVID of a person who was dying during early 2020, mid-2020, who was dying and who had no loved ones around. They and the staff of the hospital filled a rubber glove with warm water and put it on the person's body to simulate human touch. And it was the most heartbreaking thing I saw during that whole very difficult period. To your question, Paolo, we had, and again, my—the lens at which I come to this is through public bioethics, which is the governance of science, medicine, biotechnology, in the name of ethical goods. So I'm thinking about end-of-life decision making. And you imagine, in order to construct a legal framework which shapes behavior and even shapes opinions through the pedagogical mechanism of the law. So teaching us what we should think about such things, not merely reflecting what we think—the law, the mechanism of law actually does teach as well as reflect what a given people think about a particular question. You have to have an image of what the patient is. You have to be faithful to the patient that you have in front of you right now and all of the complexity that he or she is experiencing in his or her vulnerability. And unfortunately, what becomes the forgetfulness of the body manifest in the end-of-life law comes up by constructing a legal framework that simply exists to maximize autonomy at the end of life, which is in some ways a category mistake when you're talking about a patient who's incapable of making autonomous decisions for him- or herself.

We're in the midst of experiencing a wave of dementia patients because of aging. The way life, the shape of life has changed over time, in many respects, for the good, because of advances in biomedical science and care. There's an enormous and growing population of people suffering from dementia. And of course, there are always people who suffer from other cognitive impairments that make it impossible for them to take care of themselves. And of course you have children who can't make decisions on their own behalf. If you're imagining a human being as merely a bundle of desires and willfulness, and you're trying to fit that square into round hole, you're going to create structures that can't respond to the full neediness of the person in that particular moment.

I'll give just one small, concrete example in the context of assisted suicide, where it's debated in its state-by-state question and different states have legalized assisted suicide. About 10 or 11 states, maybe 12, have legalized suicide, and all of the laws are based on the original statutory framework that Oregon passed in the 1990s. We know that suicidal ideation is highly correlated with treatable mental illness. A super-majority of people who have suicidal ideation suffer from reversible clinical depression, or at least clinical depression you can treat, especially if you have cancer, which, again, is a huge percentage of people who try to make use of assisted suicide. Yet these laws are designed in a way not to require the psychological assessment of people when they get their prescription, and even more importantly, when they self-administer the drugs to take their own life, there's no one there. There's no concern about vulnerable populations like the poor, or the disabled, or the elderly. There's an epidemic of elder abuse in the United States right now, and in California, you may recall when they legalized assisted suicide, Jerry Brown, the governor of California, got up and said, "You know, in asking myself whether I would sign this into law, I asked, What would I want at the end of *my* life?" And what he was imagining was himself, at this moment, privileged, powerful, white, making a decision on his own behalf to write the last chapter of his life. That's not the reality. Most people don't go to the doctor at the end stage of life seeking to "maximize their unencumbered will." They want someone to help them and to take care of them, and he was asking exactly the wrong question. The question isn't what the powerful governor of California wants at the end of his life. It's, What do poor people need? What do the disabled need? What do the elderly need? What do stigmatized minorities need? Because those are the fragile populations, owing to their embodiment or sociocultural circumstances, that require not freedom alone. Of course, they need freedom, but not freedom alone but also the protection of the law.

That is an example of misunderstanding what a patient is and operating according to an idealized standard, according to a framework which I talk about elsewhere, called expressive individualism. We'll talk about it later, but it captures what we're all talking about right now, the idea of the disembodied will, the idea of the individual whose highest flourishing is to interrogate the depths of his or her own sentiment and then follow their original life plan. That's what human life looks like, they think, not the messiness of total dependence and vulnerability. We all begin our lives utterly dependent upon others. We, in the very best case scenario, follow a gentle arc of life upward to the height of our powers and then immediately pivot backwards, downwards to total dependency again, and expressive individualism only gives an account of the person at the very peak of that arc, and for only the most privileged and powerful.

Paolo Carozza: I mean, I love the way both of you have really brought out in different ways how the weakest and most vulnerable are the ones who are going to be most directly impacted and affected by these kinds of shifts and distortions of what constitutes our humanity. But also, it strikes me that underlying this seems to be a very distinctive understanding of what freedom is, that is quite distorted in a certain sense. I mean, what does it mean to be free, and how does that relate to this sense of whether the body is something to be valued and an integral part of who we are, ontologically as beings or not, or something that can be separated? Is there something? What does it do to our sense of freedom? How does a distorted sense of freedom drive this problem? And how does the problem contribute, perhaps at both an individual level and at a cultural level, to what our understandings of what it means to be free and a free society? Any thoughts about that?

Christine Rosen: Well, the conceit of the technological project is that you are free in embracing it. And by that, I mean that living a lot of your life online on platforms and in worlds designed by others to sell you things, to get you to behave in certain ways, to keep you on the platform, that is its only purpose—that that's a new and liberating form of freedom. This was the bill of goods that we were all sold when the internet came along. And I think what we have to think about now is, What is freedom for? Because what the technological project wants us to ask is only, What are we achieving freedom *from*? What things do we dislike as human beings that we'd rather not have to deal with? I'd rather summon a car with the press of a button, never talk to the driver and be dropped off at my location. I would like to have my food dropped on my doorstep again after having summoned it on my phone, never having to look in the eye the people who prepared it or delivered it. And then, if you look at the demographics of our country right now, you'll probably eat it alone while watching other people doing things on a screen.

A lot of conversation recently has been about the loneliness epidemic, but I think that is misleading. We have an epidemic of self-isolation. We're choosing this. We're choosing to live in a way that we think is freedom, but freedom only can happen and flourish for the most number of people possible if it comes with obligation. And I think what a lot of our technology, whether it's at the beginning or end of life, we assume for ourselves a level of control that is false, because when everything breaks down and your body fails you, you will suddenly have that lesson taught to you in a very harsh way, and you might not have the moral and psychological fortitude to deal with it.

I think we are raising generations of people who literally can't look someone in the eye and have a conversation without feelings of great anxiety, and that is not merely a problem—it's a tragedy for human interaction, because that's not what we're supposed to be doing if we're raising our children and grandchildren in healthy ways.

Look at the rhetoric of the technologist, Mark Andreessen, for example, a big venture capitalist. He talks about reality privilege, the idea that if your reality is terrible, don't try to fix it. That's not going to happen. You can live your life online instead. You can have freedom and control online, in these worlds that give you vastly greater opportunities for creativity and emotional resonance. This is the promise. *He's* not going to live in that world. *He's* going to live in *his* reality, which is quite nice. In fact, he and his friends are building a private city outside of San Francisco where they can all live. You know, more power to them. But the reality that they see for most of the rest of us is one that's deeply unfree. It is designed by others to control others. That's not the freedom that I think we assume we have when we pick up our phones and order something from DoorDash.

Paolo Carozza: Great, great examples. Carter, you've thought and talked a lot in your work about the centrality of dependence and a recognition of dependence to the human being and to human flourishing. How does that relate to the question of freedom that Christine was mentioning?

Carter Snead: I mean, everything Christine said is beautifully said and exactly right. I mean, I was imagining what you said about the notion of friendship, of freedom in this technological context. Because "technological" is intrinsically "instrumental," or something that relates to rational mastery and power. It's a language of freedom as directly related to power and control, control of your own circumstances. But as we all know, we live in a world interconnected to other people. The world of expressive individualism is not merely a world of collaboration among disembodied wills. It's also a world of strife where you have to overcome the wills of others just to realize what it is that you want to do to build the sort of virtual life that you want to have.

And Christine mentioned in that context assisted reproductive technology. I got to know Christine in the early 2000s, when I was working with the President's Council on Bioethics with all of our wonderful mutual friends, and we were working on a report called *Reproduction and*

Responsibility: the Regulation of New Biotechnologies. We asked an expert—I won't name him, because I don't want to shame anybody—to come and tell us what genetic screening for sex selection and trait selection and hair color and eye color, and now for IQ—what is all this for? What is genetic screening for? He had six weeks to think about it. He came and sat down in front of our council and he said, "It's to help parents realize their dream of a disease-free legacy." That was the phrase.

That's a very specific kind of freedom that he's talking about, the freedom to pursue your dream of a disease-free legacy. Now, the strange irony of that formulation is it had the word *parent* in it, because a parent is a relational concept. There's no such thing as a parent without a child, or at least a hoped-for child, and that relationship of parent and child in his framing is one of instrumentalization, rational mastery. Which is not to say—I mean, please do not hear me saying that people who use assistive technologies come with that perspective. It's not at all the perspective they come to the table with, if they come to the table with the perspective of profound vulnerability, because their bodies have failed them. Their bodies have failed them, and what they most want is to parent a child of their own flesh and to love a child of their own flesh.

But what the law does in the United States, and really the absence of law, is to create a framework in which that profoundly vulnerable group of folks are led into and tempted into making decisions about quality assurance and selection of sex and skin color and eye color and IQ that transforms the relationship between parent and child, which *should* be the ultimate network of uncalculated giving and graceful receiving—into something else. Leon Cass said a child is a mysterious stranger that we welcome and we love unconditionally. A child is a gift that stands in relation to you on equal footing, equal dignity. But if a child is made and not begotten, that distorts the perspective of what a child is.

Again, I'm not talking about the perspective of the parents or even the practitioners. I'm talking about the perspective of the law. If the law tells you a child is a product, then that's a deep problem, because that's not what parents want, that's not what they need. Yet they find themselves without guardrails and without anyone to support them other than this highly commercialized industry that approaches them and offers them all these things. It offers them a disease-free legacy.

Christine Rosen: Carter's making such an important point. The law is doing one thing, and the practitioners are sort of trying to offer whatever new, latest technology they have on offer, thinking this is the best thing for their patients. Then there are all these social pressures that bubble along underneath all of this. But inform the parents, inform the practitioners, and certainly inform the lawmakers, which is this assumption that this amount of control is fine, but—and this is true of all technology—it doesn't tell you what's *not* on the menu, right? Kids are like, I can get anything on my phone. I'm like, Well, look at how this has been structured. What *aren't* you allowed to choose?

So you're a woman who's pregnant, you're above a certain age, and your OBGYN says, Well, you have to have an amniocentesis to check for Downs. And if you don't want to do that, you have to put up a fight in many cases. So that's not on the menu anymore, even if your obligation to your child is to love it unconditionally regardless of how that child comes into the world, as Carter says. Anytime we embrace this new "technological control" way of thinking, we take things off the menu. And many of the things that we've taken off the menu, whether it's with regard to how we build families, or whether it's how we just go through our daily lives, has taken those qualitative things off the table. We have a lot of *quantitative* options, but the moral and ethical responsibilities, the *qualitative* emotional experiences—helping others and feeling a deep and lovely sense of obligation to others—that's off the menu in a lot of cases. We have to fight for it. We have to demand it now.

Carter Snead: And the virtues that you need to flourish as an embodied human being, embedded in networks of giving and receiving are missed as well. If you think of life as a consumer, you're not thinking about the virtues of uncalculated giving, just generosity, hospitality, *misericordia*, which is accompanying others in their sufferings. Or the virtues of graceful receiving, gratitude, openness to the unbidden—you know, tolerance of imperfection. These are all things that are—and again, all these virtues can be understood through their lens of genuine friendship, hoping and seeking the good of the other without counting the cost to yourself. And if you're thinking about everything in your life as a drop-down menu to order the thing exactly as you want it, then you're irritated when you get something that you didn't ask for, and DoorDash brings you the wrong thing or doesn't bring the sauce with your burrito or whatever, you know, you have a kid, and this isn't what I hoped for. I was told that my child would have a higher IQ than this. I was told that my child would not have Down Syndrome. Again, it's not that this is how parents see the world. I'm talking about how the law pushes you, and culture pushes you in a particular kind of mode of thought, and you have to fight it, like you said. I mean, friends of ours who decline amniocentesis, if they're pregnant after a certain age, and the doctors are like, "What are you, religious?" Like, that's the question you get.

Paolo Carozza: So the references that each of you have made both to this question of quantification and where that fits in, and also to this sort of selecting, choosing, the willfulness of making myself that you're referring to, Carter, leads me to a question that on the surface might appear paradoxical in this discussion, and I want to get at it by asking, like, Okay, if we're separating what a human being is in this vision from the body, then what do we do with the body? Right? There's a certain paradox in the cultural moment that you're describing, I think, at least that I observe, and that is that at the same time that we're talking about a disembodied worldview and ethos, people are obsessively concerned with their bodies, right? It's all about the quantification of the body. It's all about wellness. It's all about the latest hack that is going to make me live perfectly this particular day in a physical perspective. How does that relate to the underlying problem that you've been diagnosing in your works?

Christine Rosen: It's a sign of the hollowness of our sense of ourselves that we seek to cheat death. We seek to cheat aging. It's very popular in Silicon Valley. There are companies that will argue that you can cheat death. They're trying to find ways to upload consciousness. You never have to really die. There are, in my opinion, quite horrifying apps which, if a loved one dies, you can give every text message, voicemail, video snippet and email that that person ever wrote, and they will devise a chatbot to talk to you in your dead loved one's voice. So this then robs us of the ability to grieve and to understand that there are beginnings and middles and ends, as Carter was saying, not just to the lifespan, but to our own relationships throughout our life. So I would say that it's not exactly a contradiction or a paradox. It's a sign of hunger for meaning and purpose.

So you think about these young people who spend a lot of time on Instagram, and there's this weird little phenomenon where they filter their faces so much before they post their picture that when they look at an actual mirror, they're almost unrecognizable to themselves. So it's not even the mirror of Narcissus, which was the original concern with a lot of social media. It's a strange sort of emptiness of self, like I don't recognize myself, so that, to me, is a much more concerning problem down the line, because a sense of selfhood, a real grounding in community and in the physical body, are all interlinked. If you remove one piece of that puzzle, you get people who become very confused about, not just where they belong in the world but who they actually are. Why? What is their purpose? Why are they on Earth?

I'm sounding quite existential at this moment. There's not just one simple solution, but there is a way in which we need to reframe our understanding, not just of ourselves and individualism and the opportunities, freedom, and community, but the habits of mind we form on a daily basis that lead to expectations about ourselves and others. And for that, if you spend eight hours a day staring at a screen, that's how you form your habits.

Paolo Carozza: If I can jump in for just a second before turning it back to the same question, back to you, Carter—Christine, probably the first thing that grabbed me about your book, and then made me know that I wanted to read it, was the title itself, very portentous, the extinction of experience and the reference to experience. I just want to highlight that, because in the comments that you made right now, you really bring out that the question of experience is a question of meaning, and not just of things happening to us in an external way. And so this question of how the disembodied life is a reduction of the meaning of our daily existence and the capacity to grasp that meaning in its fullness, seems to me, really at the very heart of what we're talking about today.

Carter Snead: I agree. It's what you're talking about. When you were talking, I was thinking about the Lotus Eaters and sort of narcotizing yourself and being happy. If your reality is terrible, then just opt out—virtual reality and so forth. It is paradoxical, because when we think about embodiment, and you think about the relationship between the embodied exertion and work, and the consequences of work, and how that actually enhances a person's understanding of flourishing and identity and disentangling work and embodied exertion from outcomes—like when you use anabolic steroids or something like that, it has a kind of disembodying effect, even though it takes place in the locus of the body. It's not you, right?

So there's a real salutary effect living in the world of experience, doing Aikido, mowing the lawn, whatever, like actually living as a body can remind us about our fragility and vulnerability and our dependence. But what you're asking about, Paolo, is something different. This obsession with focusing on the body and its appearance is a kind of curation for a virtual audience more than for the sake of flourishing as an organism, right?

And so the deep problem is, if you view the world through the lens of expressive individualism, in which you are disembodied, radical will—it's dualistic, like it's my mind and my will and my desire is me and everything else is instrumental. Then your body becomes a pure instrument to the realization of the projects of the will. Also in the same way that your relationships become instrumental, including familial relationships, the dream of a disease-free legacy, for example, or when your relationship with your grandma, who's elderly and frail, becomes an obstacle to the realization of your vision of expressive individualism. And so my view is that the paradox isn't a paradox if you think of the body as a mere instrument and expression of the will itself, and especially in these virtual spaces that Christine knows so much about. If we think of the body as us, then you have a very different relationship to exertion and self-improvement than if you think of the body as a palette on which you're constructing your original, authentic truths that you then display to your virtual audience.

Christine Rosen: There is an irony there, right? Because you think about how people are constantly presenting their self and tweaking their appearance to look exactly like they expect others to like, because other people have liked someone who looks like this. That's why every single actor and actress in Hollywood is starting to look the same. It has a homogenizing effect. It's not radical individualism. Even though we're like, "I'm in control. I can do whatever I want to myself," everybody ends up looking like the same version of a bot. It's very strange.

Carter Snead: It comes back to the question of freedom, then, right? My wife is telling us about a thing called Mar-a-Lago face that's real. It has to do with cosmetic surgery. All these people, men and women, end up looking alike, and it's totally weird. It's like they're wearing a mask. It's homogenized.

Paolo Carozza: Well, we could go on for a long time diagnosing other areas—like education, for example—but in the interest of time, and to avoid starting everyone off on just the dark side, sorry, we have to begin with realism, right? But we're also called to hope. And, you know, as that beautiful introductory video showed us and urged upon us, here—where we are—can begin a new life, right? Part of that is remembering the body in the literal, eternal sense of remembering—bringing the body back together, giving it flesh, making it part of the unity of who we are as human beings. Where do we begin to do that? Like, what? Where? How do we resist this? How do we address it at a personal and cultural level? What can we begin to do in our communities, in our own lives, our families, our relationships, to overcome this pull toward the dismemberment of our very selves?

Christine Rosen: At the individual level, you always choose the human—choose the face-to-face. Embrace the idea that this will be inconvenient and annoying, and you have to put on clothes and pants and get out of the house and go see your friend and wish them happy birthday to their face—not just because Facebook reminded you it's their birthday. That's really difficult. And that means, parents, when you're pushing your kid in the stroller, don't be looking at your phone—talk to your child, even if your child is pre-verbal and just grunting and pointing at trees. These daily moments are the building blocks of human interaction, and it's how we train each new generation to understand how to be human. I mean, basically, for those of you who have kids, you know preschool isn't going to teach your kid to read—it's going to try to civilize these little tyrants who are, you know, adorably focused on dominating any space they're in, in their charming way.

So, we have to do that at the individual level. But at the level of society and culture, we do need to start asking tougher questions of ourselves. This is where the law comes in—and I think Carter would agree. I mean, in bioethics, there's plenty of room for greater regulation of these things. We need to protect kids right now. Although I'm a fan of the free market and entrepreneurialism, when it comes to our children, if we know something's harming them, we change the law to protect them. And we need to do that with things like social media platforms that were designed for adults but are being used by eight- and nine- and ten-year-olds.

So, I think there's a way culture and law can work together. You can have top-down solutions but also ground-up solutions. Schools going cell phone-free are another example of this—parents are demanding it, teachers want it. I'll give you one little glimpse: I have two Gen Z sons. They're in college now, and there's this thing they do when they go out. None of them have any money—they're college students—so they go to some place for dinner. Everyone's supposed to pay their own way, but sometimes they'll all put their cell phones in the center of the table, and anyone who picks up their phone has to pay the entire bill. They're lashing themselves to the mast because they understand the appeal of that device. To me, that's a beautiful example of hopefulness. They've been raised in a culture where their expectations were formed by something they now understand to be potentially harmful, and they're trying to find ways around that. So, at all those levels, I think we just have to have more awareness and thoughtfulness about the world we want to live in—not just the one we happen to be living in now.

Carter Snead: Yeah, that's really great. It's funny because expressive individualism can't make sense of children. It imagines children are just little adults—you want to maximize their autonomy as little adults. And that's—anybody who's ever been around a child understands that's not it at all. It's funny, I was just thinking about my almost three-year-old. His name is Giovanni Battista—we call him Gigi or Baby G—and he'll grab something and say, "Mine! Bottle!" And I'll be like, what? Why are you speaking German? First of all, domination sounds better in German, maybe. In any event.

But back to the question you asked, Paolo, about the law. Those of us in law tend to think about grand solutions—like, how can we engender an anthropology of embodiment in the culture through law? And I do believe that law and politics shape culture, for sure. But that temptation, in some ways, needs to be resisted because the real answer is: the only way you can recover this is by loving the person who's right in front of you—unconditional love, self-emptying love for the person who presents themselves to you right now, responding to them in their embodiment, as a gift, as a person to be cared for—not as a project or part of my narrative to plug into something.

So, you think about these radical acts of hospitality. I think about Mother Teresa—she says the reason we have so much trouble in the world is because we've forgotten that we belong to one another. The idea of belonging to one another, even to people—it takes some moral imagination to understand how you belong to people you don't know, or that you see lying on the street, or that you see in a wheelchair, or someone who doesn't look like you. But it seems to me that, for our part, to recover a genuine vision of friendship and embodied love and hospitality is through the practice of it. And, as Christine said—it's in your interpersonal relationships. It's, you know, talk to somebody, interact with somebody, give somebody a hug—with their permission. But it's also about living in the world and interacting with those who are immediately put in front of you.

Yes, grand strategy—yes, we should think and talk about an anthropology of embodiment in our politics. When we debate and deliberate over regulatory frameworks or statutes or whatever, we should be mindful of the reality of what a human being is and what human flourishing is. But there's no mercy at a distance. You have to make a choice to live an embodied life in exactly the beautiful way Christine put it.

Christine Rosen: Can I add, please? A lot of people—certainly, I'll only speak for the technologists I've studied in Silicon Valley—they claim to love humanity, but they actually don't like people, right? So, always keeping that distinction in mind as we use the things they create for us should be helpful.

Paolo Carozza: I want to flip the same question from a different angle. Because I don't understand from your books, our conversations, or anything else you've done that either of you are opposed to technology as such, right?

I want to be clear that this isn't a screed against technology or the use of technology or the importance of technology in our lives. Human beings are as much meaning-seekers as we are tool-users—that's always been true, and technology always changes us and changes our society. So, if we think about it as a question of how we should affirmatively relate to technology—instead of thinking about what constraints we should put on it—how would we think about it? What are the ways our attitude and our relationship to the technology in our lives could be transformed or made different in a way that doesn't stunt or atrophy this more integral sense of humanity we're struggling with right now?

Christine Rosen: Okay, don't laugh, but we should be more Amish. Keep your zippers—don't become Amish—but be like the Amish. By that, I mean, no, we shouldn't stop the incredible entrepreneurial development of a lot of these things, which are going to save lives. Even in the case of things like AI, right now, one of the most amazing breakthroughs is helping radiologists better read scans and find illness in ways the human eye can't. These are remarkable things—examples of human ingenuity in the most intimate spaces of our lives, our actual physical bodies and those of our loved ones.

However, we need to ask some very pressing questions about every new thing, because Americans love our new stuff, right? We have an almost religious fervor when it comes to technology—and historically, this has long been the case. What the Amish do before they embrace any new technology is go through a list of their values. How will this change the way we interact at home in the evenings? Well, the telephone will bring conversation into the home with more people, but then we won't leave the house to talk to them either—so let's put the telephone outside the home. We don't need electric light because there's a kind of community we have at the end of the day, after a hard day's work, that suits our values and morals—so we don't need that.

But they ask the question; we don't. And I know you didn't want to talk about education, but I see this especially in education, where every new technological tool is offered to teachers in classrooms. They say, "Oh, you'll have a little AI bot that'll track each student's progress in real time and help them." That seems really neat, but what are we not asking about that? What will it take away in terms of a teacher's face-to-face interaction and what they can pick up from a student? What data is being collected that might compromise the child's privacy? What does that look like?

At the end of the day, we have to ask: What is this replacing? Because, in some sense, it is a zero-sum game. I don't like to see the world that way, but when it comes to technology, one thing replaces another. The car replaced the horse and carriage, and now none of us need a buggy whip—fine, we've embraced that. But I don't ever want to see a world where my smartphone FaceTime conversations replace going to visit my elderly neighbor who just needs some human companionship. I could do it on FaceTime, but it's better to take the trip out into the real world, in my physical body, and sit with her.

That's where I think we hesitate—because we love the ease, the convenience, and the efficiency of all these devices—to ask those tougher questions. Look, we'll ask them about nuclear power and AI, but what about the first thing you touch in the morning and the last thing you touch at night? For many people, it's their phone. So, we need to ask if that's the world we want to live in. That's something I think the Amish and other more isolated communities—just how they do things—can teach us. We can learn from that in terms of building worlds that reflect our values.

Paolo Carozza: Fantastic. Carter, last word?

Carter Snead: As usual, I agree with Christine. So, I'll make it concrete in the context of assistive technologies. For example, what do you ask? The question is: What are parents and children, and how can we serve a relationship characterized by uncalculated giving and graceful receiving that holds intact, with integrity, the vision of a child as a mysterious stranger you welcome and love unconditionally—that a child is a gift, not a product or a project? Then, when we're presented with new forms of assisted reproductive technologies, we ask: How does that add to or take away from that vision of what parents are and should be? How does it threaten the human goods we most care about?

So, if you're asked about a technology that predicts the IQ of this embryo versus that embryo—and we're going to destroy and literally end the lives of those embryonic human beings who fall below a certain IQ threshold, or aren't a preferred sex, or whatever—how does that choice, that technology, relate to the proper relationship between parents and children, what a parent is, what a child is? That should inform our judgment about how we support those technologies or not.

Paolo Carozza: There's so much more I want to ask you, so much more to explore. I'm sure that's true for our audience, too. The good news is that both Christine and Carter will be available afterward at the Human Adventure Books table—starting now, I think—to sign copies of their books. You can explore a lot of these issues in those as well. I'll also close by saying that conversations like this happen because the New York Encounter is such an amazing and unique event. But it only continues if we're all a part of it. So, please be generous with your donations. Outside, there's a place where you can do that; you can also do it online at thenewyorkencounter.org/donate. Please be as generous as you can. But for now, unfortunately, I have to bring this wonderful conversation to a close. Please help me in thanking our guests today.

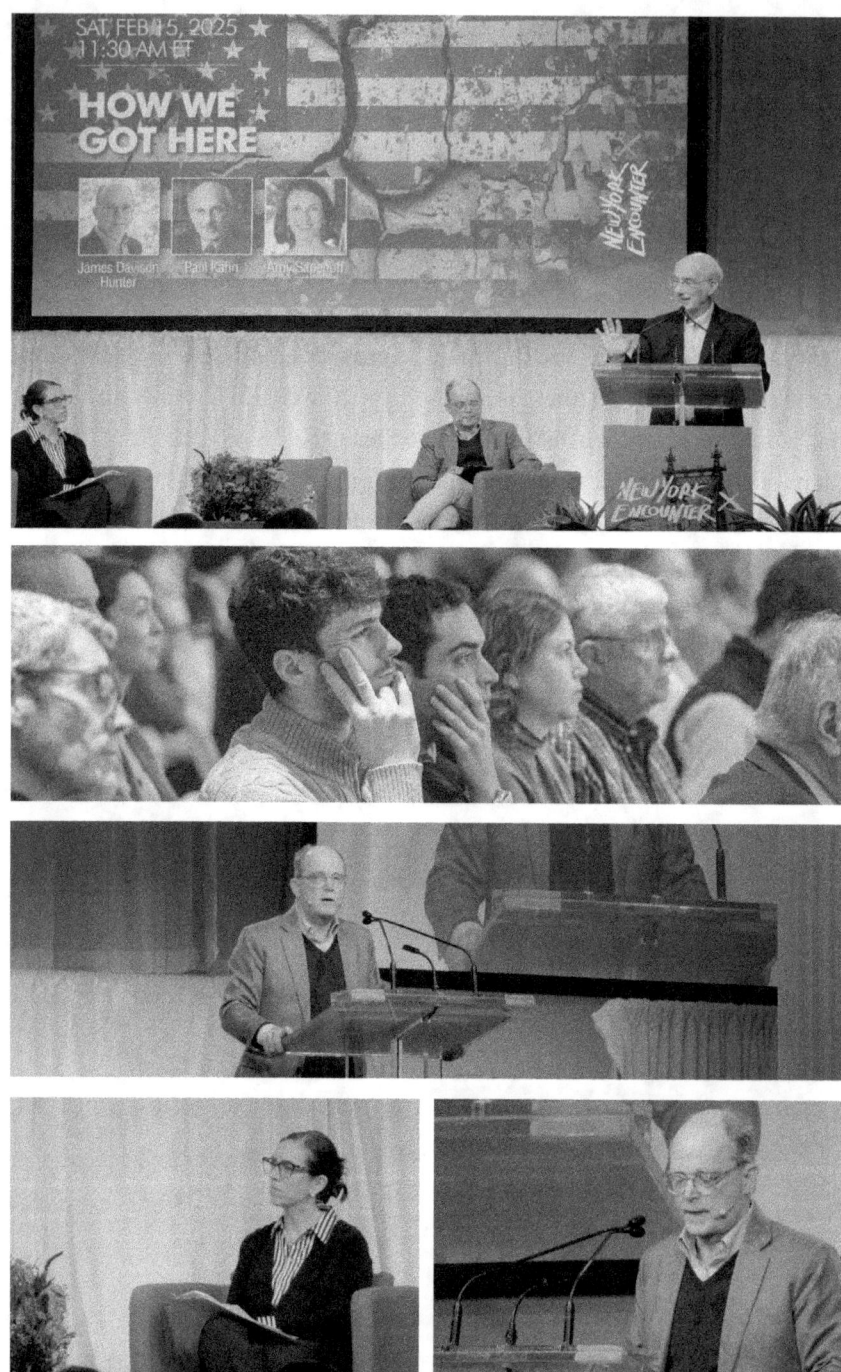

How We Got Here

A discussion on the roots of the American political crisis with **James Davison Hunter**, Distinguished Professor of Religion, Culture, and Social Theory, University of Virginia, and **Paul Kahn**, Professor of Law and the Humanities, Yale University. Moderated by **Amy Sapenoff**, teacher.

Introduction

According to opinion-makers, half of the country thinks the other half is not "really" American (and vice-versa). How did we arrive at this deep-rooted polarization whose end is not in sight? Where do we need to point our attention and energy to address this? Both speakers tried to answer these questions in their recent books. They argue that the true problem is not polarization per se, but the absence of cultural resources to work through what divides us, on the one hand, and, on the other, the increased difficulty for citizens to take part in their community's collective life. Their conversation will be a fascinating attempt to identify the causes of the stand-off and, thus, offer more adequate ways to address it.

☧

Amy Sapenoff: Good morning, and on the Encounter's behalf, welcome everybody—those present here in an embodied way at the Metropolitan Pavilion, and also those of our friends who are joining us online from the live stream at home. My name is Amy Sapenoff. I teach high school American history and American government just outside of Washington, DC, and I was thrilled to accept the invitation back in the fall to moderate this panel. Since then, I've only been overcome by a sense of dread. Perhaps I share some feelings with the people here in the audience today, but the complexity of our political crisis and trying to make sense of everything that's transpired in these past few years has only made the question of how we got here more urgent.

Thankfully, we have an incredible panel of speakers today to help us tackle this question. We're going to be a little unorthodox in terms of our format here. Both of our speakers are going to be making a few prepared remarks from the podium, but for the sake of time and efficiency, I'll go ahead and do both introductions now.

On the far side of the stage we have James Davison Hunter. He is the LeBrosse-Levinson Distinguished Professor of Religion, Culture and Social Theory at the University of Virginia. Since 1995 he has served as the executive director of the Institute for Advanced Studies in Culture. He has written 10 books and published a wide range of essays, articles and reviews, all variously concerned with the problem of meaning and moral order in a time of political and cultural change in American life. His most recent work is *Democracy and Solidarity on the Cultural Roots of America's Political Crisis*.

Sitting immediately next to me is Professor Paul Kahn. He's the Robert W. Winner Professor of Law and Humanities and a director of the Orville H. Schell Jr. Center for Human Rights at Yale Law School. He earned his PhD in philosophy from Yale University and his JD from Yale Law School. He served as a law clerk to Justice White in the United States Supreme Court from 1980 to 1982. Before coming to Yale Law School in 1985, he practiced law in Washington, DC, during which time he was on the legal team representing Nicaragua before the International Court of Justice. He's the author of 14 books, the last of which is *Democracy in Our America: Can We Still Govern Ourselves?* I invite you to check out their full biographies on the New York Encounter website, but first, join me in welcoming them. We will begin with Professor Hunter's remarks.

James Davison Hunter: Thank you, Amy, and thanks to the organizers and the volunteers who make this ideas festival such a wonderful event, and thank you all for coming today.

We often think of democracy as a given, a stable institution of modern life that works more or less to our liking, more or less effectively. But right now, of course, most Americans see their democracy as broken, but they see it in a particular way. They see the problems of democracy residing within politics itself—that the crisis of democracy is really a crisis of the other side. If we want to fix this crisis, we just need to vote the other side out and the right side in. Or else we approach this in a more technical political science way: we need to fix the primary season, change the Electoral College, put an end to gerrymandering, or just try not to be so polarizing in our politics and public discourse.

Most of us want to believe that American democracy is fixable, and we believe that we can do this if people of good will will only try harder. But what if the problems are deeper? What if the problems are not merely technical or political, but historical and cultural? This is the premise of my argument in *Democracy and Solidarity*. The central question of this book is this: How does an Enlightenment-era institution, liberal democracy, survive and thrive in a post-Enlightenment world? I want to take my 10 minutes to try to unpack that question.

Modern democracies don't emerge out of nothing. They emerged at a particular time and place in the sweep of human history. Modern democracy is extremely unusual. The context within which modern democracy emerged was Europe and North America in the late 18th and 19th centuries, at the time of the powerful intellectual and cultural revolution we call the Enlightenment. The great democratic revolutions were the offspring of the Enlightenment.

But it's important to note that the Enlightenment in France, often thought of as the model of the Enlightenment, was in fact very different from the Enlightenment in England and Scotland, and they were different still from the Enlightenment in Germany. All of these were different from the Enlightenment in America. Here, it was distinctive by virtue of being a hybrid Enlightenment. It drew from a number of different sources, a blend not only of neoclassical thought, but Lockean individualism, a Whig tradition of history and political philosophy, and a very prominent strain of Reformed Protestant or Calvinist Christianity.

Why does this matter? Democracy is not just a set of political institutions, but more fundamentally, it is a moral imaginary and a complex of social practices. This moral imaginary and those social practices were drawn from the Enlightenment and in America, our particular adaptation of it. From these sources emerged an ethical vision for the reconstitution of public life, a vision of greater freedom, equality, and toleration, but also a vision that was tempered by interdependence, sympathy, neutrality, and benevolence, and such civic virtues as loyalty to the community, knowledge of public affairs, civility and restraint in the conduct of deliberation. This ethical imaginary was novel to history, which is why the founders called it a *novus ordo seclorum*, a new order for the ages, a new beginning for humanity.

These cultural sources not only made these ideals and ideas intelligible to ordinary citizens, but in the process, they also provided sources of solidarity or cohesion in a diverse population that could contain the public's many internal disagreements. The instruments of democracy—its political institutions, its rituals and practices—were not that vision of the public good, but rather these institutions served it, supported it, and in these respects, gave political expression to it.

The problem with America's hybrid Enlightenment was that it was beset by contradictions. From the outset, we promised freedom to all, but then denied freedom to large swathes of the population. We promised equality to all, but refused equality to vast portions of the people. We promised to tolerate differences, but then were deeply intolerant of many of the differences that are constitutive of life, meaning, and identity. These contradictions played out widely, not only against the aboriginal tribes of the continent and African-born slaves, but also against Roman Catholics, Mormons, and Jews. Ultimately, the questions at stake in these contradictions was who was an American, who was included in the American project.

The larger part of the story I tell is how, over many generations, we Americans worked through the difficult contradictions inherent to the hybrid Enlightenment in the effort to create and sustain a more perfect union. Through these tense, conflictual, oftentimes violent processes of working through these differences, the hybrid Enlightenment evolved, became something different than it was before, but all in ways that were still recognizable to the past. These cultural sources remained more or less vital, at least until the present.

The questions and contradictions of American life continue unabated. We are still asking the question, who is an American worthy of its rights, protections and responsibilities? But now we no longer have the resources to work through them. The cultural assumptions and ideals that have long underwritten liberal democracy have now lost much of their normative grip. Put differently, the cultural antecedents of liberal democracy in America—those assumptions and social practices that have long made our politics vital—have largely dissolved, and all the efforts to reconfigure and revivify those cultural sources are proving profoundly deficient.

More troubling still, there are signs today that the sources of the hybrid Enlightenment are being replaced by a very different and much darker imaginary and cultural logic, which is why the cultural war has become so incommensurable. There are simply no obvious solutions to our political conflicts, for there is now no shared framework or cultural logic, or sources through which antagonists could settle their disputes, much less reasonably contend over the meaning of America's past or present, or reasonably chart a shared future. Implicit in it all is an incapacity to answer the question of what it means to be an American in the first place.

Neither faith nor reason nor their early Enlightenment synthesis can now resolve the concrete and enduring political questions made pressing by the advance of modernity. Who can enjoy the benefits of freedom and equality? What are the limits of toleration, and on what grounds do we reconcile various personal, private and factional interests with a public good? And perhaps most elusively, what is the public good in the first place?

The political stalemates of the early culture wars were challenging, to be sure, but now they have evolved into warring hegemonic projects defined by a competing will to power. On the face of it, our political system is still very Jeffersonian—it's recognizably Jeffersonian—but underneath it, around it and through it, our political culture is now Nietzschean, which is why annihilation, "cancellation" to use another word found on both the right and the left, is not an accidental feature of our political culture. It is the point of it.

So here we are. The question I posed at the very start of my comments comes into sharper focus. How does liberal democracy, an Enlightenment-era political institution, continue to thrive and survive and constructively evolve in a post-Enlightenment culture? Is there anything that remains of the hybrid Enlightenment that might be salvageable or renewable? What if anything can be reconstructed from this deconstructed culture? Or if salvaging the hybrid Enlightenment is neither possible sociologically nor desirable politically or ethically, then what encompassing ethical vision could underwrite liberal democracy going forward? What credible authority could establish the factual or moral truth of matters or could command the respect and assent of the majority of citizens? What *telos* could bind Americans together in a common hope? What *mythos* or common story could reunite Americans in all their differences? And given that the culture war has riven all the institutions of civil society—institutions of faith, primary, secondary and higher education, philanthropy, the news and entertainment media, the law, professional associations in every field, and now even corporations—what institutions could be the carriers of this vision, this story, this hope?

From its earliest years, American democracy was understood as a grand experiment in constructing a novel political order upon a new foundation. American democracy was an exercise in hope, namely, hope that the world and the lot of ordinary people could be made different and better through a liberal democratic political order. Yet experiments can fail and hopes can be dashed. We are certainly at a moment in history when the answer to the fundamental question about the vitality and longevity of liberal democracy can no longer be assumed, though not because we are politically fragmented and polarized, but because we no longer have the cultural resources to work through what divides us. Thank you.

Paul Kahn: First, thanks to the organizers and everybody working on this event for inviting me, giving me the opportunity to speak and participate. I'm looking forward to the rest of today and tomorrow. I thought I would respond to James by trying to summarize three or four points that I see slightly differently, but aligned. I think the main difference between James and myself is he's a sociologist and I'm a lawyer, and so he probably wins in this audience in terms of respect.

But I think a lot about these issues, and I think a lot about what ails

American political culture. On these things, we mostly agree, but I bring a slightly legal perspective, so I'm going to pick up just four ways of thinking about the things he mentioned, and say some very brief things—more categories that maybe we can pursue.

First, James began with the idea that everybody believes American political institutions are broken. Everybody's trying to figure out what kind of a fix might be available, and hoping it's an easy fix in the sense that maybe if we just adjust the primaries, that'll be the trick, or maybe if New Hampshire doesn't vote first, that'll be the fix, and everybody's got their list. I think that there's a fundamental flaw in this sort of thinking, which is a flaw in the way in which democracy is thought about. Too often the assumption in this country is that democracy is about voting.

In part, a robust democratic system has, in my view, three elements of which voting may be the least important. What is the first? The rule of law. Democracies operate according to law. We can come back to discuss what's the primary object of attack right now—law, democracy is in trouble. First is the commitment to the rule of law, to the idea that institutions make law, that we're committed to law, and that law has a certain longevity and certain ways of proceeding and a certain process of recognition, and that we're all equal before the law. Absent law, you don't have a democracy, you just have a mob. That's the first element: law.

Second, democracy is committed to a certain moral vision. You don't have a democracy unless every individual is treated with equality, dignity, and respect. It's not a democracy when one party wins and it immediately subjects the other party to disregard, immorality, and scapegoating. So you need these two elements, which are foundational: law and the morality of individual dignity. Then you have voting. But voting is only a means for picking leaders. It's a decision mechanism. It's not the essence or truth or measure of democracy. Historically, our leaders were very worried about this—democracy as voting without the ethics of dignity and the rule of law, which is just mobocracy. Why should a majority govern if it abuses a minority?

That's the first point. We need a more robust idea of democracy, and it's the thinness of our idea of democracy, identifying it with voting, that is in part getting us into confusion about what's at issue here.

Second point. Historically, we have worked through the contradictions between our deep cultural commitments and the contradictions of those commitments, and that assumes that our institutions have been capable of taking on that task. One thing that I think today—and we can talk about it some more—is that American institutions are primarily 19th century institutions, late 18th century, 19th century institutions. What the hell is the Electoral College? The question is whether these institutions are compatible with 21st century forms of construction of public opinion. Can you really have democracy constructed as ours is with these 19th century institutions, in a world in which the cell phone is a dominant form of information providing, in which TikTok is where people get their news? Our institutions are based on ideas like deliberation, one-to-one engagement, commitment to enlightenment values and enlightenment beliefs.

We have to think about whether we have the set of institutions that's capable of allowing us to work through these problems today. We see that, of course, on stage right now, where most of our institutions seem to have just gone quiet. The Senate is supposed to be a great deliberative body. I don't think it's doing that at the moment. How do we construct institutions that are actually responsive to the ways in which we live our lives today? That's the second problem.

The third problem goes to James's point about each of the parties expressing itself as a kind of warring effort to take control, to exclude the other, to display itself as a powerful entity. I don't know what James would think about this, but I think James famously invented the idea of a culture war. Well, I want to famously invent the claim that it's no longer a culture war. We are in the middle of a *civil* war. It's not something we worry about in the future. We're in a civil war now and it's important to understand what a war is. A war isn't just a display and use of violence. Violence is a tactical decision once you're in war. Wars have long periods of peace or non-violence. Ask the Ukrainians, what are they worried about? Ceasefire doesn't end the war.

What is a war? A war is a situation in which our institutions are no longer capable of resolving our problems. When there are conflicting groups that don't have any institutions by which the problems between them can be decided, you're in a situation of war. That's international relations generally. IR theorists say there's always a state of nature, a state of war between countries, no institutions. Then the decision whether to use violence or not is just a tactical decision within that. That's where we are. Our institutions cannot resolve our problems.

The Supreme Court says via the *Dobbs* decision that *Roe* is over. Nobody on the opposition says, well, the Supreme Court's decided; right now, we have to support the decision. Instead they say it's not really law. The decision itself exacerbates the conflict. Think about the 2020 election. Biden wins the election. What does Trump say? And the Trump supporters? "He's not my president. He didn't really win." The decision exacerbates the conflict. We're in a situation in which our institutions are no longer capable of deciding, in the sense of making a decision for all of us. They just take sides. That's the perception. In that situation, violence is always a tactical possibility. Of course, many people are scared right now that violence is on our agenda.

Fourth point. I think that the central faith of American life, the thing that held everyone together was, of course, law. I'm a lawyer, sure, but it was the following belief about law that held us together: the law is the product of a popular sovereign. We make law together. Law expresses our political identity, and it's a political identity of participation in a collective, intergenerational, transtemporal agent. That's why we could think the Constitution is our law. It's not that some dead white guys produced it 250 years ago. We produced it. They just drafted it. We produced it. We are the authors. This idea that we are all members of a political community as a collective agent that produces law as our own—that's what held us together.

We can talk about the conditions under which that belief can be sustained, but that's been the central belief in American life. I would go so far as to say that this belief, the belief in popular sovereignty as a source of American law—was a source for which generations of Americans were quite willing to sacrifice themselves. This is the story of American political life as an ultimate transcendent meaning—that belief was the religious foundation of American life. I say that belief in a transcendent, popular sovereign was a successor religion to the classic monotheistic religions of the West.

In simple terms, for many people, God died at the end of the 19th, beginning of the 20th century. I say he was replaced by a new god, the popular sovereign. What's disturbing America is a failure of faith. No longer is that faith making a claim on young American citizens. Why? Well, we can talk about that some more, but it has to do with almost everything cutting away at that faith. So those are my comments.

Amy Sapenoff: There is a lot to work through. There was already a conversation that was starting in the green room before we came on, and I'm excited to dig in here. I think this final point that Professor Kahn was making is maybe the best place for us to start. We both acknowledge that there had been some shared vision of public life together, that there was a conception of a popular sovereign that was able to hold us together. It's clear that this unifying principle no longer animates our shared political life, our communities. I'd like to pick up the conversation there, with Dr. Hunter.

James Davison Hunter: Well, secularization does fit into the story in interesting ways. Nowadays, we take for granted the kind of Lockean and Jeffersonian distinction between private and public. Part of the story of American exceptionalism is that of all the modern nation states, religion thrives here in ways that it hasn't thrived in most of the nations, at least in northern Europe, Canada, and elsewhere. It is a nation, as one historian put it, with the soul of the church.

The proliferation and vitality of religion, especially in the late 19th and into the 20th century, was mainly within the private sphere. Through so much of the 19th century, the distinction between public and private really wasn't boldly drawn. Claims were made about the ordering of public life. They're reflected in the history of law and the history of certain parts of constitutional law. I'm thinking of the definition of marriage, for example, against some of the claims of Mormons at the very end of the 19th century.

But the most interesting part of this is what happened at the end of the Civil War. Both north and south were making very bold claims about the designs of Providence, the sanction of Providence over the war effort, both in the south and in the north. Someone was going to be wrong, and it turned out to be the south. This most bloody and devastating of wars, this most economically devastating of wars, in a way undermines the authority of any religious body, any religious community, any theological tradition to make absolute, or at least bold, strong claims about the ordering of public life. As Mark Noll has put it in his argument about the Civil War as a theological conflict, religion could no longer make those kinds of public claims.

Ever since the Civil War, religion has continued to thrive, but it's no longer been able to make the kinds of credible public claims without deep contestation. I think a big part of what emerged in the early years of the contemporary culture war was the frustration of, in particular, conservative Protestant and conservative Catholic communities about things that were going on in public life in America and the sense of being muted, of no longer being able to express the deepest convictions about how the public order should be. This is what Neuhaus, of course, called the naked public square, and that served to be a source of great frustration. Increasingly it motivated many on the conservative and religious right to start asserting claims out of these theological traditions.

What's most interesting now, it seems to me, is that in the culture war, very few people are making theological justifications. The Christian right has now become widely secularized. It doesn't even try to justify the kinds of things that are going on now on their side of the political divide.

Amy Sapenoff: Professor Kahn, I invite you to respond, but I also want to ask a related question in a more targeted way based on something that you wrote recently about this idea of the popular sovereign and what we lose when there's no longer a transcendent understanding that's attached. One idea that I found interesting was that when there's an incarnational sense within the popular sovereign it generates a capacity to think about sacrifice as a part of democracy and democratic shared life together. I was wondering if you could pick up on that idea. What does sacrifice offer in a democratic project?

Paul Kahn: Let me make a few points and come around to that. First of all, I'm deeply skeptical about claims of secularization. Not that I don't think secularization has happened, and surely secularization of America's traditional religious forms, religious institutions, has happened in big ways. As James says, after the Civil War, and then into the first part of the 20th century, there's a decline. I trace this in my book about Killingworth. If you look at the first 200-250 years of Killingworth's history, it's very hard to distinguish between the Congregational Church and the political community. They're deeply intertwined with each other, and that influences all your thinking about things like participation and volunteerism. It's not really meaning the same thing when you're doing it in front of a congregation as it is when you're doing it in front of a secular community.

But the 20th century and its phenomenon of nationalism must, in my view, be viewed as a religious phenomenon, and in part, that's sacrifice. What is the 20th century? It's one mass mobilization and war after another under an ethos of sacrifice. We don't do that for reasons of commercial advancement. It doesn't make any sense to sacrifice your children so you can get a fancier Toyota. It doesn't make any sense unless we understand that the state is making a kind of transcendent, ultimate claim upon us that only works if there's a response to the claim that people have to understand this as defining something that's bigger than themselves. It's trans-historical that has a presence in their lives that they want to pass on to their children. To understand the 20th century, which is the bloodiest century in history, we have to take seriously the movement of faith to what, from the traditional church point of view looks like secular institutions, but which are operating effectively as a new political theology.

Something happens in the late 20th century to this configuration. One thing that happens is that the generation of the Second World War dies. There's a lost memory here to be replaced by Vietnam and then Iraq, and these are all failed efforts read as abuses of government power. So that's one part of the story. But then there's everything else that's going on in the rise of a kind of advanced capitalism, the reconstruction of work, the rise of the Internet, the development of the cell phone, the disappearance of the Fairness Doctrine. In that story, there is a role for the remnants of the traditional church. They're not very powerful, as we see. They're powerful because they have a substantial political block. They can vote, but nobody can take seriously the claims that they are an effective political force as a religious force. People who are deeply religious are actually deeply puzzled about what's happened to their political institutions, their political presence.

One of the claims I've been making for decades now is that we misunderstand politics if we think it's based on contract. This is my critique of liberalism. Politics doesn't begin with contract. It begins with sacrifice. A political community arises when there's a commitment to defend and express the community through sacrifice. That's the distinguishing element of politics as we've traditionally understood it. Then one has to ask, well, what are the conditions under which we can maintain a politics of sacrifice? Some people might say, well, we don't want to maintain a politics of sacrifice. Let's call that peace. Of course, I'm all for peace, but I think what's distinctive about politics as the kind of community and values that we know is that sacrifice is always at the edges.

I and James and most of you, we've lived our entire lives under the threat of mutual assured destruction, and that, it seems to me, cannot be ignored. What is the nature of the political community that allows it to say that there are possible confrontations in which we believe it's better to end history than to continue as our political community? That's the puzzle that has to be explained when we think about politics. The welfare state comes after that. When you think about the conditions of belief in which that's a possibility, then you have a very rich discussion of the sort that James points to. What is the culture here? Where does it come from? What's it drawing on? How does it borrow from its religious tradition? How does it understand the tasks assigned to it? And for me, how does it understand its sacred script, its constitution? How do we interpret a constitution that has to support that weight of a transcendent claim upon us?

I think it's very fundamental. If you ask me what's the crisis today, I would say all of that's dying, and we need some kind of alternative understanding that can support a serious politics. That's a million dollar question today.

James Davison Hunter: If I could just respond quickly, part of what I think is a fairly minor disagreement here actually is explained by a conceptual or definitional difference about what is religion in the first place. In social theory, there's a distinction between the substantive and the functional. I don't disagree with you at all—the kind of authority that I was speaking of and the secularization that has followed from that is about substantive religious communities. But part of what emerged out of that was still the remnants of a very powerful civil religion that was about the religion of the nation itself. It was certainly substantive in part, but it was also functioning like a kind of public religion.

Part of what has disappeared is the powerful functioning of that civil religion—that too seems to have disappeared. What is replacing it is a kind of hardened political religion, a political theology in which political ambitions themselves become the god, the transcendent. It's part of the reason that accounts for, in my opinion, the sort of utopian tendencies, both on the left and on the right, that have made a certain kind of politics a religion that is exclusive of anything other than the most pure form.

Paul Kahn: I don't agree with the last part of it, but I do agree with the first part of it. As you said when you started, American politics takes place in a rich cultural context that is dominated by religious and enlightenment belief. No doubt about it. It's not an accident that we are a culture, a political culture that puts a text, and reading a text, at the center of our lives. That's not an accident. That comes from somewhere, the idea that you organize a community around reading an ancient text. So the role of law and our understandings, our ethical understandings of inclusion, struggle over who's in—these all have rich religious roots, and they outlast, in my view, those religious roots, in some ways, in the sense that we have a common political, ethical morality. Maybe we don't see it at the nation level, but if you go to our local communities and our enterprises like this, you see great convergence on the ethical ideas that come out of this tradition.

All of that's true. I agree completely that there's great stress on those commitments and those values. We live in an anxious age, an age of insulation, isolation, an age in which people are questioning those values. All of that's true. The only quibble—and it's not really a quibble, because doctoral theses are being written on it as we speak—is: How do we understand this transition in the 20th century? I'm inclined to say, well, it's not really secularization. First, there's a great investment of, let's call it the religious energy, the capacity to define a meaningful life into politics. That gets us through the middle of the century and the Second World War. Then things begin to fall apart. In part, they fall apart because the courts take this idea very seriously. Under that idea of leading the nation in the development of its deepest ethical commitments, we start getting *Brown v. Board of Education*, and then we get *Roe v. Wade*, and one thing after another. The courts, which had not been a major element in this set of commitments, becomes the leading edge.

There's a story about how law became the background commitment to the leading edge, and then it becomes the focal point of political, cultural opposition. When *Roe* passed 7-2 in the court, it wasn't thought of as a major case. In many ways, Justice Blackmun thought the big case of the year was one about the antitrust applications of baseball. For a conservative movement that had organized its opposition to the developments in American law and American progressive culture around opposition to *Brown v. Board of Education*, they realized that's not going to work. *Roe* was their opportunity, and they've been very successful organizing themselves around it.

James Davison Hunter: Part of the problem here is that law is the language of the state, ultimately. Because the underlying consensus and the popular sovereignty was—did not form law. At this point, it was not forming law. Law was used as an attempt to impose a consensus on a nation in which there was no consensus on abortion, and there still is no consensus on that question. The same was true again in the 19th century with the *Dred Scott* decision. It was an attempt to impose by force of law at the highest court of the land. Also, by the way, centered on a text, and by men and women who wear what look like religious robes and work in a building that looks like a temple.

But the problem was it hadn't worked through the problem of unequal humanity. The same is true, of course, with *Roe v. Wade* and the *Dobbs* decision, which reverses *Roe v. Wade*. We are just as divided as we have ever been, because popular sovereignty's no longer forming the law.

Amy Sapenoff: I'm going to interject there and add another question that maybe will get us to a higher level thinking about these things. This concept of working through—and I think that certainly we would say that given the polarized nature of the highest levels of politics and government, that there's no capacity there to work through, that working through is much easier at the local level and amongst communities. I'm wondering if you could speak briefly about the need to think about political relationships at a more local community level, in order to reclaim some hope of this possibility of working through.

Paul Kahn: Well, I like the way you pose the question very much, because it's always important to me to recognize that America is not falling apart in many ways at the local level. States are a little more complicated, but there are local communities everywhere that are working through their problems. This craziness of American national political life in this division does penetrate into the local ,and that's a big problem. But when community members sit down together and address common problems, they appeal to a necessity of common sense, and they have the resources. So the crisis at the local level isn't that there aren't resources to work through the problems. The problem is that people are paying less and less attention to it. They're committed to other things. They're off at work 20 hours a day, or they're commuting, or they're busy with their families and managing the sports teams and all of this stuff. So the problem is one of drawing people in. It's not to recreate a set of values that has somehow disappeared.

The big problem, I think, is to tthink about the institutions, the cultural and normative set of resources and taking it up and saying, we have to create institutions in which people can act well, and interact in a way that appeals to their common sense and addresses real problems. I think there's a large majority of the American people who want to do this. They think what's going around them is crazy. They really don't like the chaos. They would really like to figure out how to do this.

How do you do that? I joked before about this, saying, hey, let's shut down the internet. I don't think that's going to happen. But there are vast structural forces working against the train. Mind you, not just here. This is an important thing to remember when you think about the problems of American politics at the moment: it's happening everywhere. So if we limit ourselves to what happened here in the last election, we aren't going to grasp the problem of politics in contemporary life.

I can say a few things, but they're very general. One is, we need political leadership that responds to this, that understands this. We need political leadership at the local level that understands it. If our kids, our students, are not being trained in the ethics of politics in schools, then they're learning their politics online, which is like learning sex education from pornography sites. So the schools have to, instead of fearing talking about politics, be deeply engaged with politics.

Point number three, I think it would be great if we went back to conscription. Is that going to happen? I wouldn't conscript people into the military, but I think it's a great idea to take young people and say, you have to do a year or two of public service. They're too young when they go to college, anyway. Last I heard, we are *firing* people in the federal government. We aren't hiring them. But these are the sorts of things that could begin to draw upon the ample normative ethical sources that exist in the country, and begin to address the pathologies of national politics.

James Davison Hunter: Well, we don't disagree at all on this point. Part of the problem, I would say, is that America is just too big. Democracy works in local communities. It works in cities. It works at the state level, and oftentimes at regional level, because it's focused on solving problems, and the problems are deeply felt by everyone who lives within these localities. It doesn't matter whether you're on the right or on the left, whether you're conservative or progressive or religious or non-religious—people are living through these problems, and the problems have to be solved. There's a level of accountability that happens at the local level that is simply not happening at the national level. America is just too big.

The other thing I would add here is that in the research for this book, I found over 400 organizations that are committed to addressing the problems of polarization, of trying to bridge the gap between the left and the right. I am 100% behind these initiatives. The problem is that there is a grand canyon between these local initiatives and the kind of initiative of communication strategies that happen at the national level.

Our public and political discourse is dominated by what happens in social media and by the efforts of major news media organizations, social media, and so on. It is sustained by conflict. It is sustained by creating, by making extreme statements that are not mediated, in which there is zero accountability and that are not oriented towards solving problems. It's a symbolic politics as opposed to a pragmatic politics that happens locally, and that demands responses, demands accountability. So the question for me is, how then do you scale up into the national? Right now, it seems to me that most of the traffic between one side of the Grand Canyon and the other side is the seepage from the national down to the local, where Twitter then becomes the medium by which we relate to each other, communicate and try to solve our differences, in which, again, it's not about solving problems.

Amy Sapenoff: Well, unfortunately, in order to pursue those questions further, we'll have to invite you both back next year. Instead of how do we get here, we'll ask, where are we going? And we'll see what happens. Thank you very much, and again thank you to our speakers.

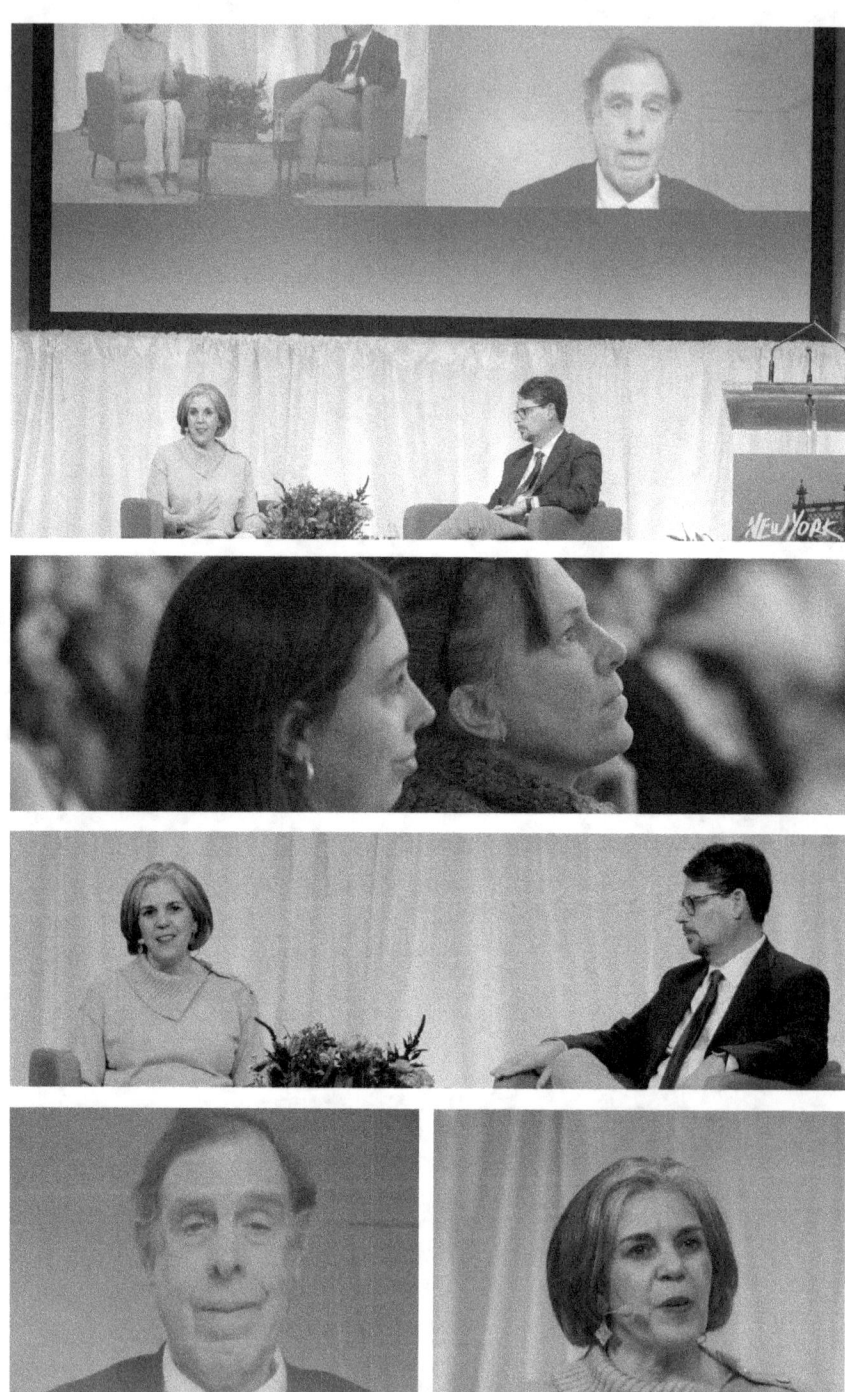

WHY HAVE CHILDREN?

A conversation on demographic decline with **Nicholas Eberstadt**, *Henry Wendt Chair in Political Economy, American Enterprise Institute, and* **Brad Wilcox**, *Professor of Sociology, University of Virginia. Moderated by* **Margarita Mooney Clayton**, *Associate Professor of Congregational Studies, Princeton Theological Seminary.*

Introduction

One current phenomena drawing attention is the steep decline in worldwide birth rates. Is this demographic drop-off a real problem when overpopulation has been presented for years as a real threat to our future? What are the most predictable consequences for society? What might be the main causes and most adequate remedies? These are some of the questions that the speakers will address in their conversation.

✠

Margarita Mooney Clayton: Good afternoon, and on behalf of the New York Encounter, I welcome all of you—both here at the Metropolitan Pavilion and joining us online—to this panel on "Why Have Children?" My name is Margarita Mooney Clayton. I teach in the Department of Practical Theology at Princeton Theological Seminary, and I'll be your moderator today. I've had the pleasure of knowing Brad Wilcox from the University of Virginia since we were both graduate students in Sociology at Princeton just a few years ago. He is the Jefferson Scholars Foundation University Professor of Sociology and the Director of the National Marriage Project at the University of Virginia. Professor Wilcox's research focuses on the quality and stability of marriage and family life in the United States and around the globe. He is the author or co-editor of at least five books, the most recent of which is *Get Married: Why Americans Must Defy the Elites*, and his research is regularly featured in outlets such as *The Wall Street Journal, The Atlantic, The New York Times,* and National Public Radio. Nicholas Eberstadt will be joining us online. He holds the Henry Wendt Chair in Political Economy at the American Enterprise Institute (AEI), where he researches and writes extensively on demographics, economic development, and international security, specifically in Korea and Asia. He is the author of several books and regularly appears on major TV networks. Mr. Eberstadt has a PhD in Political Economy and Government and an MPA from the Kennedy School of Government at Harvard, a bachelor's from Harvard University, and a master's from the London School of Economics.

To get us started on this wonderful question of "Why have children?" I'm going to turn first to Mr. Eberstadt, who's joining us online. He'll kick us off with a general question: What is this demographic drop-off? For so long, the discourse around population was that the world was overpopulated and that was the greatest threat to our future. So, thank you for joining us, Nicholas, and please get us going on this question of the global depopulation problem.

Nicholas Eberstadt: Thank you very much for inviting me to this important gathering. I'm delighted to be with you. We're not used to thinking about the low-income world as being a replacement-fertility zone, but the world as a whole is now a place where maybe three-quarters of humanity lives in countries where childbearing levels are not adequate to maintain population stability. Since we know that rich countries are only a small fraction of the world, this means that the overwhelming majority of low-income families are now sub-replacement. I think this is a big surprise for many people, but we've been overtaken by the facts in this area. All of East Asia is now in the midst of deep population decline. For East Asia as a whole, fertility levels are only half of what would be needed for replacement populations. If you go down to Southeast Asia, almost every country there is below replacement—even recently developed countries like Myanmar. India is a below-replacement society. If you go to the city of Calcutta, which was listed as overcrowded half a century ago, you'll find that birth levels are one child per woman per lifetime. We could keep circling the globe with this. In Mexico City, birth levels are below one baby per woman per lifetime. For the first time since we started collecting figures, birth levels are lower in Mexico than in the USA. The same is true with Colombia, Chile, and Brazil. One number that astonishes me is Bogotá, Colombia—the birth numbers there are down below one per lifetime. We were aware an overwhelming childbearing revolution was happening in the United States and Canada, but it's not just there.

Margarita Mooney Clayton: Well, thank you, Nick. I'll say it's quite shocking—or surprising—to think that in some of the examples you gave, like Calcutta, there's basically below-replacement fertility, which means the population will decline. We're used to thinking about that maybe in Europe or perhaps the United States, but if I heard you correctly, you said three-quarters of the world now consists of countries where the population will effectively be declining. Let's continue with some more information that Brad will share with us, and then we'll dig into the "why" behind these trends and what this means for us.

Brad Wilcox: Thanks, Nick, and thanks, Margarita. I want to turn our attention away from the globe for a second and focus more on the story unfolding in the United States. Certainly, one of the most proximate dimensions of this dramatic transformation we're seeing in fertility is the fact that love and marriage have fallen on harder times of late. What I describe in my book *Get Married* is that the American heart is closing. We're obviously seeing less dating, less mating, and less marrying here. For instance, we've seen the marriage rate drop by more than 60% in the US since 1970. That might seem like a relatively abstract number—what does it mean in practice for the young adults here today, of whom there are many, as I've noticed? Well, it means that about one in three young adults in this country—folks in their early 20s—are projected now to never marry, to be permanent bachelors or bachelorettes. We've never been in a moment, culturally and demographically, where so many people will go through life without the benefit of having a spouse or being married. That's one manifestation of this closing of the American heart, and it has obvious implications for the subject of today's conversation. The fertility rate in the US, partly as a consequence of this decline in marriage, has fallen dramatically in recent years. We're now seeing a fertility rate in the US of 1.6—well below the replacement rate of 2.1 babies per woman. But again, what does that mean for the young adult population more generally today? As this slide indicates, we're projecting that one in four young men and women today will never have kids. That's a lot of folks never experiencing the burden—but also the blessing—of being a mother or a father. These are, I'd say, manifestations of this closing of the American heart.

Now, it's important to understand that there are scholars out there—like Eric Klinenberg, who teaches pretty close by at NYU—who would minimize these trends. They'd say this is a manifestation of how we, as a country, are giving people more freedom to live their best lives, often as single people. His book *Going Solo* does, I think, a pretty good job of articulating that perspective. But as you might guess, I think he's off the mark. In a nation marked by rising economic inequality, in a society that's increasingly addicted to what I call electronic opiates—and we all know what I'm talking about here—at a time when many younger adults are beset by loneliness, I think marriage and family actually matter more than ever for the welfare of not just kids, but also adults. Particularly in a context marked by greater economic inequality, more technological distractions, and growing atomization, having the benefit of a spouse and children is even more valuable for Americans—adults in particular—than it was in earlier decades.

I'm talking about people like Scott, whom I profile in my book. Scott has a lot going for him by contemporary standards: a graduate degree, a good job, a six-figure salary. As I spoke to Scott, who lives in the outer suburbs of Washington, DC, he talked about how he feels like there's no one there for him. He's not married, he doesn't have kids, he's in his mid-30s. He comes home every evening, does the same thing with his dog, and he worries about what might happen if he gets sick later in life. There's nothing to anchor his weekends—no spouse to hang out with, no kids to take to soccer or football. All these things are absent from his life, and he betrays a certain sadness as I speak to him. Scott's experience is by no means an outlier. Social science data on contemporary life shows that fewer Americans are reporting they're happy with their lives—the classic

Declaration idea about the pursuit of happiness is waning. One recent study from the University of Chicago finds that the most powerful predictor of this decline in happiness is that fewer Americans are finding their way into marriage and family life. Then there's the issue of deaths of despair—more Americans are dying from drug overdoses, suicides, and alcohol poisoning. The data shows, again, that the biggest predictor of this trend is that fewer Americans are embedded in a marriage and family context. Finally, when it comes to the health of the American Dream, Raj Chetty's work shows that in communities where marriage and family life are weaker, kids' odds of realizing the American Dream—moving from poverty to relative affluence—are much lower. So, I'd suggest this afternoon, as we discuss this subject, that the fact that marriage and family life have become much harder for adults is having profoundly concerning consequences unfolding around us in this contemporary moment.

Margarita Mooney Clayton: Thank you, Brad. I want to follow up on what you and Nick opened with and think about some causes of this lower fertility and global population decline. You've mentioned marriage rates, but Nick, I'd like to turn back to you for a moment. Your work focuses on economic development and international security, but you've also written about labor, work, and responsibility. What led you to notice that in places like Korea or India, the population isn't replacing itself? When you present this research in those contexts, is this phenomenon a concern to policymakers? One could say decreasing populations have happened historically—through war or plagues, unfortunately—but this decline seems to be happening by choice. Could you tell us more about how, in your work at the American Enterprise Institute, you turned your attention to this question of population, and what policy-level responses you get when discussing this in places newly facing population decline?

Nicholas Eberstadt: Well, Margarita, I started working on global populations back when I was an undergraduate in the 1970s. The intellectual flavor of that decade was a terror about what was called the "population explosion," as world numbers were increasing at a rapid tempo. There was a sort of anti-Malthusian consensus in much of academia and policy circles that it was essential to bring down birth rates and encourage smaller families in poor countries. This was based on a really shoddy and fundamentally flawed analysis. It wasn't as if we suddenly started breeding like rabbits—what actually happened is we stopped dying like flies. The increasing world population was driven by a health explosion—and if you have to have a population problem, a health explosion is a pretty good one to have. This is sort of the continuing thesis of human population today. The paradox is that we've had bigger growth numbers over the past half-century than ever before. We're healthier, richer, better entertained, and better fed than any humans in history. People in economics and policy circles weren't ready to confront the possibility that, through voluntary choice, we'd arrive at a place where sub-replacement fertility became the norm and global population peaking and decline looked possible much sooner than anyone imagined. That's what seems to be coming in this century. When I go to a place like South Korea, where birth levels are two-thirds below the threshold of population stability, policymakers talk about this phenomenon, but it's a bit of a weird headline issue. They discuss it, but they don't really seem to understand what it'll mean for their society, and they certainly haven't done much to adapt to it or change it.

Margarita Mooney Clayton: Thank you. So, Brad, you've mentioned this phenomenon—obviously, there's going to be a decline in fertility if there's a decline in marriage and large numbers of people in this country never marry or have children. I wonder if you could comment a bit on the changing outlook on marriage. This morning, one of the panels featured Carter Snead, who mentioned that children remind you life isn't just a drop-down menu—you need to welcome surprises. I remembered when I lost my grandfather and was at the funeral, chatting with my grandmother. They'd raised 14 children in Cuba. I said, "Abuelita, did you always want 14 children?" She said, "Oh, no—12." I was like, "What?" She said, "Well, that was the biggest number I could think of, and look how God has provided." Back then, in an agricultural society, there was a sense that marriage and childbirth were part of nature—God would provide, and there'd be a way. She didn't have a plan. My question came from a mentality of, "I'm your granddaughter, and I need to plan this." Well, it wasn't in my plan to be one of the statistics you presented—a childless woman. I married in my late

40s to a man in his 50s, but I don't have biological children. Growing up, everyone in my family seemed to have kids, and I was the one who didn't. Thanks to you, when you adopted your first son, I hung out at your house all the time and had a wonderful time. But why this sense that, on one hand, people desire marriage and children so much they have a great plan for it, yet it doesn't happen?

Brad Wilcox: In terms of understanding why both marriage and fertility have declined in recent decades, I think part of the story is that people are actually less planful about dating, love, and marriage than they are about education and work. There's what I call a "Midas mindset" that preoccupies many younger adults—especially those higher up the socioeconomic ladder—rather than a mindset geared toward getting serious about dating and marrying. For example, two years ago, I was talking to my RA at UVA, a young Catholic guy. I asked about his plans for the future in terms of his career. He had a detailed plan: get his MBA in two years, work for a consulting company first, then do this with his career after that—very clearly mapped out. But when I asked, "Would you like to get married?" he said, "Yes." I said, "Well, are you dating anyone?" "No." "Is there any plan to get things going?" Complete silence. He hadn't devoted the same intentionality to dating and marriage as he had to his work life. So, I think part of our challenge today is that we're often focusing more on education and work.

But there are larger currents explaining why both fertility and marriage have declined in the broader culture—things you and I would call expressive individualism from our sociological training at Princeton, greater secularization, and huge technological shifts like birth control and, more recently, smartphones. Part of the story behind Nick's comments this afternoon about dramatic fertility declines across the globe is that coupling has also dropped significantly in places like Turkey, Tunisia, and Vietnam. It does seem the proliferation of smartphones—making us more distant and conveying unrealistic expectations about life and love—have played a role. These broader shifts in technology, individualism, and secularization, plus the changing dynamics between the sexes, are key. I hear over and over from younger women—left and right, religious and secular—a frustration that it's hard to find a marriageable guy who's got his act together, a full-time job, and a clear sense of his future. Part of the challenge in many countries is that younger men are struggling to mature and launch, which impacts people's ability to date successfully and marry. These factors help us understand why dating, marriage, and childbearing have become more vexing and challenging, both in the US and elsewhere.

Margarita Mooney Clayton: So, part of what I hear you saying is that markers of being a responsible adult have shifted to career and work goals, which people can articulate and pursue. But I wonder if we could turn to Nick for a moment on this phenomenon of social media. I've been hearing lately from Jonathan Haidt, a social psychologist looking internationally at the smartphone and the coincidence between its emergence and the drop in fertility. The picture I've come away with is that in countries like Japan or China, where fertility decline was already happening, people from one-child families spend a lot of time on smartphones and not much around others—a social context that doesn't seem conducive to marriage. Nick, what have you observed about the connection between technology, smartphones, and the drop in fertility?

Nicholas Eberstadt: I think Brad put his finger on it. This little friend here—the smartphone—is a huge technological disruptor, potentially almost as consequential as the pill. In my anecdotal travels in places like Turkey, India, or East Asia, I see people jumping through this "Narcissus mirror," living an alternative life on the other side of the screen. I'm not convinced it's a better life than the flesh-and-blood one we all have the option for. I think this will turn out to be very consequential. I don't have hard data to prove it yet—it's more an intuition—but it's striking how this acceleration in birth and fertility drops tracks so closely with the global proliferation of smartphones. And smartphones are everywhere, even in less-developed countries. Thinking about what you and Brad said, as someone trained in economics—where there's wonderful work from Nobel laureates like Ted Schultz and Gary Becker at the Chicago School, which I think is terrific—it can't fully explain the big change in "exogenous tastes," as an economist would say, that we've seen over the last generation, especially the last decade. Those are taken as given in economic training. But we've had a huge shift in tastes worldwide. I'd describe it as the rise—and maybe triumph—of a quest for autonomy in all sorts of societies. Autonomy and convenience seem to be the trump cards in family development and formation. What you're seeing is a flight from the family in search of autonomy and convenience. Children are wonderful—I can tell you that as a parent—but one thing they're not is convenient. So, we've got this flight from the weak by the strong in our society and many others. The kicker, of course, is that everyone begins life as a dependent and often ends it that way too. It's a tough sword to live by.

Brad Wilcox: One additional point to build on what Nick said: we've been getting exogenous shifts in culture, with more messaging that being a parent—especially a mother—is a route to misery, not flourishing. There was a piece in *The New York Times* by a Brooklyn writer—only a Brooklyn writer would mine this vein—saying heterosexual, married motherhood in America is a game no one wins. She chronicled her travails as a wife and mother, and there've been many pieces in this spirit, emblematic of a suspicion emerging in elite culture and social media toward marriage, parenting, and especially motherhood. In the US, younger single women now think the path to happiness runs away from family life toward being single and free. Work by my colleague Dan Cox finds that younger single women believe they're happier staying single than marrying and having kids. But they don't know the data points in the opposite direction. My work with Dr. Wendy Wang shows that, for women, no group is happier than married mothers—and the same is true for married fathers. Married moms are almost twice as likely to be very happy with their lives compared to single, childless women aged 18 to 55. For men, married fathers are more than twice as likely to be very happy compared to single, childless men. The feminist thinking in *The New York Times*, or the new-right thinking of Andrew Tate—who says there's zero statistical advantage to marriage—and this anti-natalist, anti-nuptial rhetoric, is off the mark. For ordinary Americans, being a mother or father is associated with more happiness than being childless. What's striking is that the happiness gap between parents and childless adults is growing in favor of parents. This might tie back to my earlier point about fewer alternative sources of meaning and social solidarity in broader society besides marriage and family. So, why have kids? Sociologically, it's one of the few places offering an intense experience of meaning, direction, and solidarity, with opportunities to both receive and give care—which is what makes us fully human.

Margarita Mooney Clayton: This is the question we're tackling, right? Why have children? What are the deep cultural and psychological implications of declining fertility? My mom was one of 14, and my dad was the oldest of seven from Floral Park, New York. I once asked that grandmother, "Was it hard to raise seven children?" She said, "Nah, kids come with instructions." One day, a colleague from China gave birth and was overjoyed. I went to her house to meet the baby, and she was holding it like a plate—the baby's head was whacking around. She asked, "What do I do with the bottle?" I said, "Take the baby, hold its head like this, and stick the bottle in." She asked, "How did you learn that?" She'd never touched a baby until she gave birth, and I was speechless. If what we're hearing today is true—societies with one child, 30 or 40 years between mother and child— you don't have grandmothers showing you what to do, like I did. You don't have aunts, uncles, and cousins galore, and you don't know anything about babies until you have one. But what struck me was that when my friend became a mother, nothing was more important to her than being a good mother. The desire was there, but she needed an instruction manual. In this reality where people aren't having children but desire it, is that human desire to have children still something we can activate? If so, for those who have that desire but didn't have the blessing of a big family like mine, what's the instruction? Do we need to publish a manual on how to do this?

Nicholas Eberstadt: This is terribly important. Back in the '70s and '80s, E.O. Wilson and sociobiology ruled intellectually as a fashion—the idea that we're hardwired to act like human beings. If that were true, we'd probably be hardwired to reproduce our numbers over time. We're seeing pretty heavy evidence we need to rethink that. If E.O. Wilson is out, René Girard is in—mimetics, social imitation, and social learning are crucial. My boss and much better half, Mary Eberstadt, wrote a book with an analogy to a cat stuck in a tree. When the fire department rescues it, it's always a pet raised apart from its family, lacking the social learning to get down. We've got a similar decline in social learning about large families. It's easier to burn social capital than to build it, but it's possible—especially if you frame it as a social need open to discussion.

Margarita Mooney Clayton: Second question: Do we need an instruction manual on how to hold and burp a baby? The deeper question is, what is this process? As you described, Nick, I lived it organically—being around children, learning the beauty. Every cousin's birth was a celebration. Most holidays were marked by birthdays, baptisms, or communions—events around raising children that everyone joined in. Even when I was childless—and I still am, though I have stepchildren now—I was part of raising kids, even if they weren't mine. I saw Brad's family grow from his first adopted son to his fifth, then his wife giving birth to twins, and then their eighth child. It was natural for me. What is this organic process of mimesis and social learning around the joy of children? Yes, the responsibility, for sure—but for those who don't come from my background, there's still a desire for connection, to give oneself to the next generation. Even for those in your stats, Brad, who'll be childless and marriageless, what does it mean to recover this sense of great joy and wonder at a new life, and that the fundamental thing a society can do—spelled out well in today's Hannah Arendt exhibit and talks—is come together to pass tradition to the next generation? How do we take up this call personally, but not atomistically—not individually—because it's a call for all of us to celebrate the meaning of children, the joy of new birth, and the miracle of new life? How do we do this?

Brad Wilcox: One challenge is that anyone who's a parent—or knows parents—knows there's a lot of suffering, sacrifice, crying babies, and teenage dramas. Pop culture and social media often elevate the stressful, demanding aspects of parenthood today. So, it's important to be embedded in communities that attach meaning to the sufferings and sacrifices parents make for their kids and family life. Psychologist Paul Bloom shows that suffering and sacrifice are good for us, up to a point, when endowed with meaning. Emile Durkheim, whom we both read at Princeton, shows collective rituals are key to giving our lives meaning, especially the challenging parts. Religious communities play an important role in helping the rising generation navigate family life's challenges and sacrifices, and in assisting those with little baby experience—like your Chinese colleague—by connecting them with experienced parents who can teach practical care and make sense of the challenges. My work shows religious Americans are markedly happier in their marriages and less likely to divorce, so their family context—while not perfect—is more satisfying and secure for raising the next generation.

Nicholas Eberstadt: This has to happen from communities outward—bottom-up, not top-down. It's a one-zip-code-at-a-time approach to reclaiming what we've lost too much of. It's hard to reason with someone who sees the world through an autonomy-convenience-consumer lens about what they're missing from the love, voluntary sacrifice, duty, and obligation fused into the family bond—the most important social unit in our world. Rather than inductive reasoning, a demonstration effect—where people see more of it and want more—might persuade them. One big difference between secular and other communities, or low- and higher-fertility zip codes, is optimism, confidence, and patriotism. They're bundled together—not determinants, but characteristic. Sometimes when you see it, you want a taste of that flavor.

Margarita Mooney Clayton: Along these lines of social learning—showing people what family life is like, where children are a blessing and joy—behind the global population decline stats, there are exceptions, right? Those are trends. So, my question for both of you is: In the contexts you've worked in, the US and globally, who's bucking the trend? Who's having five or six kids, and what's that experience like? A friend in Austria said having more than one kid is radical, let alone six, because society is structured around one- or two-child families. Who's bucking the trend? Brad, since you have eight kids, what's it like driving a giant van everywhere? Do people come to your house thinking, "Are you just going crazy all the time? Is your house upside down?" Then they walk in, as I do, and it's joyful and fun—kids doing homework, smiling—and think, "Wow, this is actually pretty cool." They don't just act like that when I'm there, I assume.

Brad Wilcox: There's a lot of chaos—I know there are big families here too. There's noise, stress, and financial challenges—all the things you'd expect. But what people don't appreciate is how our kids are like their own little tribe. They fight and bicker, but they also derive a lot of happiness from being with and for each other—it's amazing and fun to see. As an adult with a large family, you're with younger kids for a long time, even at 54—I still have an 11-year-old. It's empowering, inspiring, and keeps me feeling young. Every summer, I'm in the neighborhood pool with different kids over the years—there's something life-giving about it. A final anecdote: one morning, I was driving my younger four kids to our local Catholic school while my wife headed to work. We were voice-texting back and forth, and at the end of one text, my youngest son piped up from the backseat, "I love you, I love you, I love you," three times. We'd been having a pedestrian conversation, and my wife knew right away it was from her son, not me. This was the day after Valentine's Day—I'd tried to do okay the night before—but my youngest is particularly devoted to his mom. So, imagine waking up as a 50-something woman and seeing that on your text chain. That's the point.

Margarita Mooney Clayton: That's such a beautiful story. Reflecting on today's panels, Carter Snead talked about learning uncalculated giving and receiving. As a single woman, now married, I love being around kids because they're instinctive uncalculated givers and receivers—they teach us connection. They look you in the eyes, see through your stress, right to your heart—at least, that's how I've felt. Then there's that explosion of beauty—like saying, "I love you, I love you, I love you," right after throwing Cheerios with milk all over the backseat. That explosion of self-giving love, attachment, need, and openness to express this fundamental human need for unconditional love—not "Mommy, I love you so you'll forgive the Cheerios," but "I love you because you're my mother," or "because you're here with me now." Thinking about the consequences of fertility decline, I consider our most vulnerable—children, the disabled, the aging—who'd historically be embraced by large families. If it's life-giving for you to be in the pool with an 11-year-old, how life-giving is it for an elderly grandmother to have her grandchild hug her and say, "I love you, I love you, I love you"? How many are entering old age without grandchildren or children? What can we do to realize children's incredible capacity to give love—so fundamental to everyone, regardless of age or how many kids we have?

Simply being in the presence of kids, whose nature is self-giving love, is an incredible gift. How do we encounter children if it's not in our own family?

Nicholas Eberstadt: Thinking about what you and Brad just said so beautifully—it's a strange time. There've never been as many people on Earth as today, yet we see the prospect of peaking and decline ahead, and there's so much loneliness despite all these people. Why is that? Explaining to someone outside the family world what it's like to build a family is like describing Technicolor to someone who sees in black and white—you can tell them, but they have to experience it. One country-level exception to these trends is Israel, a fascinating counterexample to modernity's fertility decline. Over the last generation, fertility levels for Israeli Jews have risen—not just among the ultra-Orthodox, but also secular Jews. Why? One guess is that people in Israel want their country to have a future, and they want their families to be part of it—that's pretty beautiful.

Margarita Mooney Clayton: In the final minutes of our panel, the question is "Why have children?" How would you answer that, perhaps summarizing what's been said?

Brad Wilcox: We've all heard Aristotle's idea that we're social animals. I mentioned the "Midas mindset"—that the true measure of a person is their degree, money, or career. But Aristotle, Thomas Aquinas, and contemporary social scientists show that more important than those are our social relationships—friendships and family. Having kids offers nothing more powerful for giving life meaning, direction, and purpose—guiding them through life's early stages, receiving and extending love. Even the sufferings and sacrifices of parenthood, as Paul Bloom notes, are redeemed by the meaning and love we attach to them as mothers and fathers. That's my response.

Nicholas Eberstadt: There's a reason solitary confinement in prison is seen as cruel—it takes away your connection to humanity and reduces your own humanity. Family life changes you, completes you, maybe makes you better through the love and giving you offer. It's not a consumerist view, but family life brings meaning you can't find elsewhere—not the only source (faith, work, community offer attachment too), but it's been society's most fundamental unit since our species began. There's a social wisdom in that, carried through thousands of generations.

Margarita Mooney Clayton: Thank you, Nick. I recently told my students I'd be on this panel, "Why have children?" One student from Nigeria, pregnant with her second child, has been in my classes this year— it's been tough with a sick child at home and fatigue. When I mentioned the panel, she said, "Why have children? Because there's a great mystery inside you, growing, and there's nothing more incredible than that." It reminded me of a line from Marilynne Robinson's *Home*: looking into a newborn's eyes is the closest we can get to seeing the face of God. That mystery of a growing life, that overwhelming possibility—not a calculation of lost sleep or money—strikes you.

Thank you, Nick and Brad—this has been wonderful.

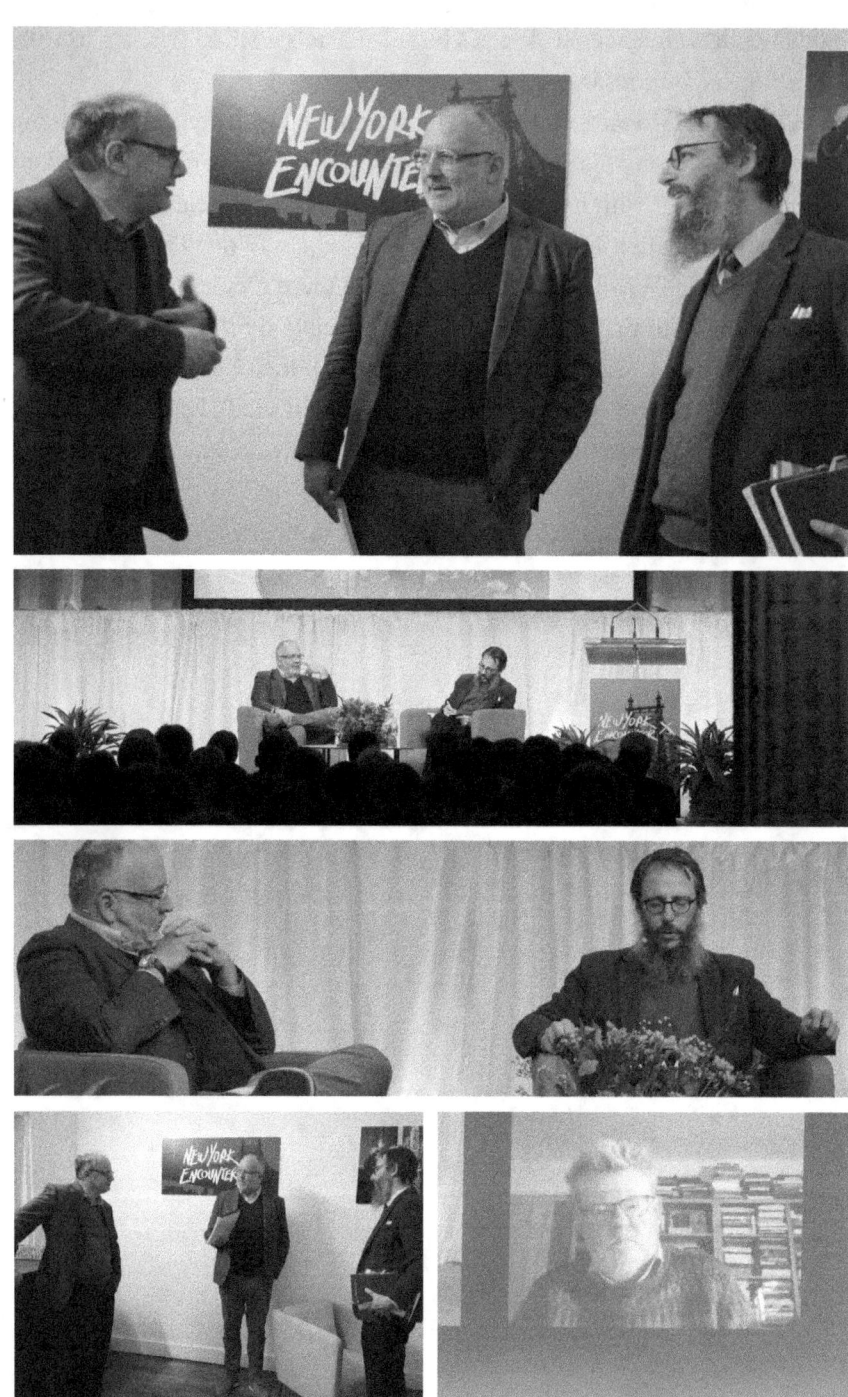

No Longer Just a Promise

A conversation on In Search of the Human Face *by Fr. Luigi Giussani, with* **Michael Hanby**, *Associate Professor of Religion and Philosophy of Science at the Pontifical John Paul II Institute for Studies on Marriage and Family, Washington, DC,* **John Milbank**, *President of the Centre of Theology and Philosophy, The University of Nottingham, and* **Aaron Riches**, *Professor of Theology, Benedictine College.*

Introduction

"The supreme obstacle to our human path is the 'neglect' of the 'I.' In opposition to such 'neglect,' an interest for our own 'I'—here lies the first step on a truly human path. It would seem obvious for one to have this interest, while it cannot be taken for granted: it suffices to look at the great abyss of emptiness that opens in our daily life, in our awareness and in our loss of memory. In fact, the constitutive factors of the human 'subject' are not captured in the abstract; they are not a 'prejudice' but become evident when the 'I' is in action, when the subject is engaged with reality. Behind the word 'I,' we see a great confusion today, and yet an understanding of what exactly is my subject is of primary importance. Indeed, this subject is at the center, at the root of all my actions (even thinking is an action). Action is the dynamic with which I enter into a relationship with everything, every person. If I neglect my own 'I,' it is impossible for my relationships to be mine, for my life (the sky, a woman, a friend, music) to be mine. To say 'my' with seriousness, I need to have a clear perception of what constitutes my own 'I.' Nothing is as fascinating as the discovery of the true dimension of my 'I,' nothing so rich in surprises as the discovery of my own human face.

And nothing is so moving as the fact that God became man to give me a definitive help, to accompany with discretion, with tenderness and power, the tiresome journey of each person in search of the human face."

— Fr. Luigi Giussani, Introduction to *In Search of the Human Face*

✠

Aaron Riches: I certainly want to warmly welcome you to this session on *In Search of the Human Face* by Father Giussani. This book is really the discovery of the experience of where a new life begins, and it's also a book that proposes the method of discovering our own humanity in the fullest sense. But before we dive in to talk about the book, I want to introduce the two people that I'm going to converse with, and maybe I should introduce myself too. I'm Aaron Riches, and I teach theology at Benedictine College in Kansas. To my right is Michael Hanby, who teaches at the John Paul II Institute in Washington, DC. And Michael and I are both intellectual children of the man who's joining us on video link, Professor John Milbank, who is emeritus professor at the University of Nottingham in England. Their full biographies are on the website. But before we really get into the book, I'd like for Michael to just give a sort of account through his own life of the mysterious thing that binds the three of us together, because I think, in itself, it's interesting and shows something of the core of what Giussani is trying to show us in the book.

Michael Hanby: Yeah, and in doing that, I'm going to embarrass John a little bit, I think. I hope he doesn't mind. I knew of John, of course, before he knew of me, when I was a master student at Duke around 1994. I think I read—it took a year, in fact, with a friend of mine to read his his magnum opus, *Theology and Social Theory*, and reading that book was an event in Father Giussani's sense. I was stunned. It overturned my world. It really changed my life. Set me on very much a different course, and opened up ways of thinking, ways of seeing that I didn't even know were possible. And I can honestly say that I wouldn't be here talking with Aaron now, were it not for that experience. As I was thinking about that in preparation for this, and in conjunction with this discourse, first of all, I should say, thank you, John, for that life-changing book, which is really what it was.

But then it also really exemplified much of what I think Father Giussani is talking about in *In Search of the Human Face*. It was a cultural event in that it helped mediate an entire way of looking, an entire vision of reality, a deeply Christian one that I didn't know existed. It was a life-changing event. And by definition, those are forever. And it helped to generate the kind of community that these events do. So something in that experience really resonated with me as I read this, because the encounter with the Mystery is always mediated. And in this case, John's work had that kind of an effect on me. And I'm grateful for that.

Aaron Riches: So my own experience is similar. Meeting John and meeting his thought was, you know, what Father Giussani says, that culture is a systematic and critical consciousness of reality, and he really helped to provide that by proposing Christianity as—how did he put it at the beginning of *Theology and Social Theory*? "The pathos of modern theology is its false humility. If it doesn't position all the other discourses, it is doomed to be positioned by them." And that is really—I mean, if Christ does not position the total way that we look at the world, then our Christianity is doomed to be positioned by some other factor in the world. Maybe John, at this point, I'm going to just let you jump in and talk a little bit about how your own work might connect with the themes that are brought up in *In Search of a Human Face*.

John Milbank: Well, I don't know what to say. That's very moving. I'm very grateful for what both of you have said, and reciprocally, I've been very, very blessed in the kind of students that have been sent my way, including both of you. I've learned enormously from them, from all of you. My wife Alison and I started going to the Rimini Meeting many years ago, after CL had made contact with me in Nottingham, as if they saw some kind of resonance between their legacy and what I was trying to do. And I think there really is that resonance, and I think it's been already indicated by Aaron, and it's probably summed up by the dominance of culture within CL, and a word that occurs again and again in the book that we're looking at. And it's funny, there's a strong link between cult and culture.

So I think a link with my thought is that Giussani definitely does not want to see religion as merely an area of life. In his book *The Religious Sense*, he sees religion as something that permeates all of life. And this might sound surprising, but I do think there's a certain commonality between Schleiermacher and Giussani at this spot, even though we wouldn't think— we often think of Schleiermacher as being sort of something of a liberal but—that powerful sense that, you know, culture often despises religion, but actually religion is at the very heart of culture.

And in the case of Christianity, that's even more strongly true, because we believe that God became man in Christ. So we think that Christ is the adequate imitation of God, so that Christ is the image of God, and then, in some ways, *In Search of the Human Face* is a very simple book in the tradition of Thomas à Kempis and *The Imitation of Christ*, that whatever else Christianity is, it's an imitation of Christ, and that through that imitation, our aim is to become Christ, as Giussani says at one point, to imitate Christ, repeat Christ again in our lives.

In the book, he insists that we see Christ in everything, and that the vision of Christ is transformative of everything else. But I think that works the other way around as well, that it's by seeing Christ in everything that we also see more of Christ. So it's also a very ecclesiological book, and I think that links up with my thoughts as well, that you can't separate Christ and the Church. And we could even ask a question that starts off—and asked if Christ was human, didn't he, as human, learn from other people, even though, as God, he had nothing to learn? As human, surely he learned from other people. And I think that's a clue to the idea that Christ and the Church are inseparable from the very outset.

And that's also part of the Marian aspect of the Church, that Christ is, in a sense, born of Mary, born from the Church. The Church and Christ arrived together, even if the Church emerges from Christ. It's a paradox that, you know, Christ, even though he is uniquely God, he is in relation with other people. Where he is, there is already the Church. And the thing that Giussani then stresses again and again throughout the book, indeed, the book builds up to the conclusion that you only fully have ethics in the Church. And that's because the Christian revolution—and you know, this is not really paralleled by anything else in late antiquity—saying you have to love absolutely everything. You have to forgive absolutely everything. You have to be reconciled with absolutely everything. There is no limit to this endeavor.

And this isn't just a vague gesture, it's a culture. It forms a kind of mysterious pattern that Christ somehow shows us, almost aesthetically, the way to do this, and even though we're repeating what he does differently, we're continuously forming this sort of Christiform shape through history. And so Giussani says the Church is—Christianity is sort of the culture of the "already has been." So it's a bit like in the video, that he insists all the time that it's about memory. You know, that unless we have this clue of Christ in the past and the way people have followed Christ, we won't see how to be reconciled with people in the present.

And you know, we've had all this argument between Pope Francis and Cardinal Sarah about the *Ordo Amoris* and—lo and behold!—there is a passage in this book about the *Ordo Amoris*. And am I right? Actually, Giussani does talk about concentric circles, and he insists that we begin love with the local but that it then has absolutely no limit in extending outwards, so that people seem to not follow the paradox that women know about, when they have a baby, they start loving all babies. You know this happens. It should be obvious, even though it's a paradox, but it seems we have this stupid battle between misreadings of the *Ordo Amoris*. And instead of that, Giussani gets it absolutely right.

And he also, at one point fascinatingly, quotes a former Archbishop of Canterbury back in the 12th century, saying that when we try to escape from the torture of our own feelings, we tend to identify with some cause of sort of justice, but those causes of justice often limit us. It's a very profound saying, I think. What we need is an extension of charity and mercy, and today, we seem to be sort of locked into either our private feelings, or we identify in a very one-sided way with some issue about justice. We don't have general sympathy. There's a decline of mercy in our legal and our public life, and I think in a very simple way, Giussani is insisting the Church is the place of absolutely unlimited love, but we can only achieve this if we remain in history and if we remain in the lineage of Christ, who showed us the perfect love of God.

So this is a really easy book to understand, and my books aren't always that easy to understand, but I think I find a strong resonance between Giussani's spirit and the spirit that I would try to encourage.

Aaron Riches: Thank you, John. Yeah, I like this phrase that you used about the lineage of Christ because it implies a history, and it implies that one of the things that I think for Father Giussani is really important, which he highlights at the beginning of the book, is what he calls elsewhere "the overturning of the method." He says people in all times seek to know the meaning of their lives and to establish a connection between the finiteness of their human face and the infinite mystery of their destiny. With Christ, the method is reversed. It is no longer the person who seeks to establish a relation with a distant God. It is God who has become a companion to that one in the most concrete and discrete way possible. And I think that this is one of the points which you're putting your finger on for us and helping us to see, which is the essential continuity between the life of this first-century Palestinian Jew and the companionship of our friendship, which is the Church, which continues now. But it also highlights the way in which our relationship to everyday life, to the banal, to the limits of life, have changed.

And maybe Michael, you want to pick this up and talk a little bit about one of the phrases, a beautiful phrase that I like, that comes up in the book. He says Christ is always found in the limits of life, and that there's nothing anymore in life that can be banal, but rather only that which is not lived attentively. I wonder if you can pick that up for us.

Michael Hanby: Yeah, I mean, I oftentimes think it's helpful to simply reverse the way we typically are inclined to think about things. And I think Giussani is helpful regarding—he refers to Christ over and over again as "the Presence," the Presence and fidelity to the Presence, not forgetting the Presence. And the idea, basically, that the reality of God is primary. If the meaning of all things is Christ, and if Christ is the really real, then there's a sense in which the Presence is inescapable.

And some of the most interesting forms of sin, which turn out to be pedagogical—I mean, I think that's one of the interesting things that he discusses in the discussion of the dynamic of sin—is the attempt, and ultimately futile attempt, to flee the Presence like a Flannery O'Connor character or something. And yet, speaking of paradoxes, the paradox seems to be that this is nevertheless something that we manage to do fairly well and fairly habitually and fairly easily. We manage not to see, we manage not to remember, we manage, by bracketing out or denying or ignoring the presence, to reduce reality to two dimensions, which I think is something interesting to say about nihilism. And I think that may be the most devastating form of nihilism, not the atheistic, sort of the inverse of Jacob's wrestling with God in the form of atheism, but rather an indifference that can't bother to disbelieve.

And how that's possible, and what is involved, the method, as it were, of being delivered from that possibility through this attentiveness to reality, reality whose ultimate meaning is in Christ, but whose meaning infuses absolutely everything. I mean, you know, going back, circling back to my original experience with *Theology and Social Theory*, and you said it very well, the idea that Christ and Christianity, by extension, the Church, has something to say and is ultimately definitive for every aspect of reality, is something that I certainly had never imagined, and I think most of us do not dare to think, because to affirm that would be revolutionary in some of the ways, and perhaps even exceeding some of the ways, that Father Giussani describes here. I have no idea whether that was at all responsive to your question, but anyway, I think it's helpful.

Aaron Riches: One of the things which you said, which I'd like to get both of you to sort of pick up and comment on a little bit—you talked about the pedagogical use of sin. You know, it seems that God allows us to sin. There's a verse in the book of Wisdom, I think it's something like "the punishment for sin is always the sin itself," or something like that. Like, you know, basically when you indulge in a particular sin, the consequence of it is precisely that indulgence. Being stuck in addiction would be a good example of that.

But he has this comment here, and this is what I want maybe both of you to comment on. He says on page 59: "One who is truly immoral is not the man who never fails, but the one who does not have this memory and

83

this passion for Christ and therefore does not reach out beyond himself." I mean, what a perfect description of my modern life, right, that I live so often without the ingenuity of looking beyond myself, looking beyond myself to another. He says that is real immorality. It's not the sin itself. And so I wonder if you could comment on that, and maybe John can comment on that too, and comment more broadly on the role of sin in the book.

Michael Hanby: Well, not only refusing to look beyond myself, but also refusing to look within myself, or, for that matter, within anything. I mean, I've written this several times, but I've always been struck—I guess it's become a little slogan of mine—but I'm always struck by the recognition that there seems to be no such thing as a profound question in American life. No such thing as a profound question in American public life. And why is that? For us to see and to think in a pragmatic, technological world, there are no depths corresponding to that. There are no depths for profound questions to correspond to, or they're, of course, there, but we don't see them.

We don't confront reality as a mystery to penetrate. You know, we confront it as a problem to be solved. And I think the beyond and the within, the depth dimension of being and the highest dimension of being are—I'm not enough of a geometer to describe what axes those operate on, but they're inseparable from each other. So this idea that Christ taking me out of myself, orienting me towards the future, it seems to me, is at the very same time, a reorientation towards the depths.

And I think, you know—I lost the line you just cited. But, and I'm going to misattribute this, I think it's Bernard of Clairvaux—you know, sin also serves. It can become, it becomes the occasion, just as the sort of wrestling with—I mean, if you think of atheism as a primitive phenomenon, say, a form of the engagement with the prior reality of God. There's a certain kind of integrity in that that might allow you to come out on the other side. And I think the dynamic of sin's pedagogical dimension, which is not a baptism of sin or justification of it obviously, but operates dynamically, or can operate dynamically in the same way that our sufferings can become a window or a doorway into a higher and deeper reality and meaning of things.

Aaron Riches: John, I want to give another quote here that has to do with sin, and maybe you can comment on that as well. He has another quotation on sin where he says, "To sin is to behave like we are the masters of our own life, and to recognize sin is to come closer to the fact that the measure, the criterion, the lordship of our life, is the mystery of God."

John Milbank: Yes, so, I mean, I agree with what both of you have said so far. I think that Giussani typically has a very sort of humane and generous kind of approach to ethics, so that the person who's simply obeying the most obvious moral rules may not be the person closest to God, because Giussani is insisting that ethics is really a matter of being constantly reformed. Once again, it's a cultural matter. He sees culture as a continuous educational process.

And, you know, the worst thing is not disobeying the rules of the school of life. The worst thing is playing truant from the school of life altogether, trying to be isolated from the ongoing process of cultural formation that is constantly aspirational. So I think this is why sin can be educative. You know, so long as you're obeying the rules, you may not be very charitable, but sometimes when you sin, you're not just sort of saying, "Well, I broke the rules," but "Why am I doing that?" And it's because there's something profoundly wrong. You're trying to be master of yourself, which is often seen as the height of being ethical. But it's not, if to be ethical is to be responsive to an infinite call, the call of other people to infinitely expand your horizons.

And you know, that's why I think Giussani thinks of the educative process which is at the heart of his thought, and of CL, as very close to the expansion of love that it's always about learning more and more and acquiring a wider and wider kind of sympathy. So, yes, I think that he definitely thinks that sin can be instructive, because being good is a total, limitless process of growing relationship and of knowledge acquired through love.

Aaron Riches: This is helpful. One of the sentences that you just said there, John, the expansion and experience of the expansion of love—when I sin, I come to grief with my own capacity to manage my life. You know, the thing I don't want to do I do, and the thing that I don't want to do I end up doing. And if I'm sincere in front of this, I come to the contradiction in me, which is the ideal, the good that I would like to do, that I know would bring me joy. I'm incapable of that. The other experience that goes with that is the experience of the presence of God, nevertheless, to me, which is the experience of mercy.

And Father Giussani has some incredibly beautiful things to say about the word *mercy*. Here he says, "The height of God's word about himself is in this supreme word *mercy*, as if God were saying, Although you are like this, I love you. You rebel against me, and I love you."

And it also connects, very importantly, I think, to the comment in the Sermon on the Mount, when Jesus says, "Be perfect, as your heavenly Father is perfect." But in the Gospel of Luke, Jesus says, "Be merciful as your heavenly Father is merciful." So it suggests that the experience of mercy, and then the experience of actually being merciful to another, that this is really the highest point at which we have a capacity to imitate and really participate in God in a way that brings the presence of who he is in his inmost self, this absolutely non-clinging, generous love, to bring it into the world. And maybe both of you, in turn, can comment on that and maybe even try to illuminate with something like an experience from your life, or something that you've seen in which it's demonstrated. Go ahead, John.

John Milbank: I was hoping that Michael would go first. [*audience laughter*] Well, I'll try to think of something. I suppose the interesting question arises of whether mercy is just something that we unfortunately have to exercise when something goes wrong, or whether, to the contrary, mercy and forgiveness somehow have a much more positive aspect to them, that maybe there's a sense in which all along, love is forgiveness and mercy, even in the absence of sin.

In some strange way, because we're always sort of making up for each other, we're always creating room for each other, allowing each other to be more giving—forgiving is somehow giving the other space to be giving so that perhaps when we forgive people, what we're doing is sort of recovering an exchange of gifts, making space for each other all the time whereby we realize our full selves, so that we're sort of recovering something more fundamental. We're not merely canceling out sins. We're sort of recovering a more primordial sense of forgiveness.

And you know, this is maybe all the difficult passages in Paul about how law colludes with sin. Somehow our whole sense that being good is about a sort of minimum of achieving a certain thing or doing this rather than that. To be in that kind of mindset, or to be in the mindset of trying to hold back evil forces is not really to be in the good. It's not to be in the sort of paradise or original innocence of goodness, so that somehow, when we're being reconciled, we have a weird sense of joy.

If we're talking about personal experiences—you know, I think we all know about this. We do something terrible to somebody else, and then we repair the relationship. But oddly, we have the sense that we've arrived at somewhere we were never at before. You know, that somehow we committed these bad things because we weren't really in a fully good relationship. So that when we have this sense of forgiving and reconciliation, there's a more radical opening up, and you arrive at a level that you feel is sort of impermeable somehow, that you've arrived at a reality that can't ultimately be damaged, even if we go wrong. In the future, we've arrived at a new level.

And I think this is where history comes into the picture, that we are in these narratives of fallen redemption, and we're always beginning from the fallen place, and it's only by repeating the forgiveness that's offered us by Christ and through the Church that we sort of arrive back at the paradisal place. And this is why, I think often, precisely, it's when we go wrong that we start experiencing radical mercy. You know, the kind of thing Dostoevsky often writes about.

Aaron Riches: Beautiful. Thank you, John. Michael, do you want to comment on that?

Michael Hanby: Yeah, I want to say something about one of the inner conditions, I think, for what John just described, which I agree with. And that is something I think that is easy not to see, because there's a tendency, especially these days of late, to set mercy and truth in juxtaposition to one another. And it seems to me that one of the things—before we get to the sin and mercy part of the book—that Giussani emphasizes is the way that the encounter, the event of coming face to face with Christ, gives us a complete, you know, it revolutionizes our vision. We now see things through other eyes, through truer eyes, including ourselves, that allows us to see the distance between the reality of ourselves and the various kinds of fictions that we create for ourselves.

I mean, the experience or the reality that John just described—it seems to me one doesn't have it, for example, without that "What have I done?" moment. I can't receive, I actually can't open myself to the reception of mercy, much less, I think, authentically give it on this higher plane, as it were, without having come face to face with the truth and seeing myself and those fictions in relation to it. I mean, this is ultimately, I think, what contrition is, or at least an ingredient of it. I think it's part of what Father Giussani is talking about when he himself talks about judgment.

And what I would want to emphasize, I think, then, is the necessary relationship between mercy and truth. If I can make an adjustment in the way that I would want to talk about this, I wouldn't want to talk about "adhesion not measure." Christian morality is adhesion, not measure—I'd want to talk about it... I mean, okay, not measure. If by measure we mean some arbitrary sort of positivist standard extrinsic to us that is a burden, rather than the deepest fulfillment of who I was created to be. But surely adhesion and a certain kind of true measure of things and true measure of ourselves, in the light of Christ, go together. And I think they go together. They obviously go together for Father Giussani as well. It's throughout the book, this transformed sense of vision and the new capacity to judge.

I don't want to make it sound as if by truth we mean something easy and completely transparent to us, and it is itself lacking in mystery. I mean, there's a depth to it that calls us further in and further on, you know, that "What have I done?" moment for one experience of this is not simply an encounter with a simple proposition or a fact necessarily or even fundamentally.

Aaron Riches: If beauty is the splendor of truth, we have an experience that the truth, when it's really looked at in its depth, is always wounding, and there is a positive aspect to that. When you see a beautiful sunset, or you listen to Poulenc play music like he did last night, you feel wounded to the point that you feel you could almost weep. You feel your unworthiness in front of the greatness of a gift that is given. And I think it creates an opening.

You never want to say directly, "I'm grateful for this sin that I did," but I am grateful for the experience of reconciliation that I have to admit wouldn't be possible had it not been for the graciousness of a God that lets me fall in order to find this—what John puts beautifully—is like a more primordial experience of love, which is mercy.

It's at the point at which the discovery that God is Love is really Trinitarian, that it has something to do with the way that the Son belongs to the Father, and the Father gives away the Son without counting the cost, and the Son gives himself back to the Father, also without counting the cost. And this is a harmonious love. It's not a mercy in the sense of a wrongdoing, but it is merciful in the sense that it is utterly gratuitous.

And I think that this opens us up to following. Following is something that happens within nature. The child follows the parent. The best education the child gets, the truest education the child gets, is just from watching the parent act and watching the parent act in relationship to the child, and the child's awareness that they belong to the parent, that they're embraced by the parents, no matter what happens.

But then there's also the history of following which is initiated by God's penetration of history, which begins with the call of Abraham. And I mean, there's a few points where Giussani talks about Abraham in this book. And to me, they're surprising and new because he looks at Abraham in a way that he sees Abraham as an icon so unequivocally of Christ that the ethical question of the sacrifice of Isaac seems to change, because I'm no longer thinking of Abraham as the father who's going to sacrifice his son and commit a sort of heinous moral act at the command of God, but I rather see Abraham as the child who's being asked to give away everything that's been given to him in proof that he belongs wholly to God. And I wonder if you and John would comment a little bit on that. Maybe we can start with John here.

John Milbank: Yes. I mean, again, I agree with what you're both saying. I suppose that the new thing that Christianity brings is this sense of the absolute finality of love, and that's bound up with the idea that the ultimate, the true and the good and the beautiful become more emphatically subjective and interpersonal than they were for the classical world. So it's as if mediation becomes ultimate. It's no longer the beginning that is ultimate. The beginning is kind of just there. It's sort of inert. But somehow the beginning was already giving itself. There was always already a middle. It was giving of by someone, through someone to someone. You know this, this triadic process so that we no longer think there is any good or true or beautiful outside this interpersonality of love—that the truth is what shows itself in the beautiful, and is interpreted as good.

So we can no longer think of knowledge in this completely objective way. It's only through loving people and loving everything that we see the truth of everything. So this is one reason why one might think that knowledge outside the revelation in Christ is limited because it's not being fully construed by love. And I think, you know, there's a real question mark about whether we've ever arrived fully at a metaphysics of love. It's something that Hemmerle talks about and suggests that Franz von Baader in the 19th century had perhaps got nearer this than anywhere else, discussed recently in a book about Louis Bouyer. I can't remember the title, but I think that, yeah, truth and mercy, they go together, but that's because we've got to think of them in these interpersonal terms of love.

Michael Hanby: I was looking for a particular passage that I thought was very powerful when I read it, where he discusses Abraham. And it's not the one on page four. I'm not sure.

Aaron Riches: Do you have it? Yeah, this is page 72.

Michael Hanby: Let's see. I'll really be embarrassed if that's not it either, then I won't have anything to say. [*audience laughter*]

Yeah, here it is: "We find a suggestion of this method first of all in the figure of Abraham, who represents the first moment in the Old Testament when God united himself to his chosen people through a promise. 'Now the Lord said to Abram, "Go from your country and your kindred and your father's house to the land that I will show you,"' Genesis 12:1. And then Father Giussani says, "And Abraham left without even knowing the goal of his journey."

And one of the things that I love about this book is the very concise kinds of exegetical, interpretive summaries that he gives. I mean, they really elicit something. And you have a sense, albeit differently, like Kierkegaard's treatment of the sacrifice of Isaac, this sense of a completed abandonment to a way that will become yours, but that you didn't originate and that you can't fully see the end of. And there's nothing of you that's left outside of that abandonment. I don't recall what your question was. [*audience laughter*] So I don't know if I'm speaking to it, but I know Abraham was in it, and this is part of what really sort of struck me about his treatment or interpretation of that.

Aaron Riches: There's a few things there. The first thing is that, in the Anglosphere, we might not be as used to Father Giussani commentating on Scripture before we've read this book as we will be after. And this is one of the real delights of this book—the amount of scripture that's quoted in here, and the comments that Father Giussani makes, which are absolutely penetrating into the scriptures in a way that is exhilarating. You pointed to that.

I think that one of the things is the way that Abraham, right from the beginning, lays up everything with God, and that's the way in which he is really a child of the Father in this sense. He lives his faith journey as a child does in the house of its parents. He doesn't worry about where he's going. He just knows that he's told to go. He doesn't worry about what's going to happen with this promise, which means more to him than anything else in the world. His son, he doesn't worry about it. He just knows that it'll be okay, and in a way that he can't understand, not just okay.

Giussani has this great line, he says, "What defined Abraham's sense of self?" And here we are, the question of the "I." You know, here begins a new life. "What defined Abraham's sense of self was that voice." And the voice, of course—I mean, it takes some thousands of years, but at a certain point that voice becomes the concrete, carnal face of Jesus, which becomes flesh and dwells among us. I mean, this is really a powerful exploration in that regard.

Michael Hanby: I remember part of what I was going to say about it vis-à-vis Giussani's own development of the peculiar, in the best sense, development of the biblical vision. I mean, he's forever contrasting the event, the encounter, with the presence and the mystery, with a mere idea or a system of thought, though, of course, as being generative of a transformed vision it issues in new ideas and new systems of thought about those things. They shouldn't be said in opposition to each other, but what the contrast captures and insists upon—and what I think he depicts so well in these interpretations—is the risk and the drama inherent in the self-abandonment and in what's being asked, and in, if you want to put it back in the terms of the discovery of the "I," in coming to discover the real meaning of your own life.

Aaron Riches: By all that Abraham lives, he says, "I belong more to you, Lord, than I belong to myself. I belong more to you, Lord, than even what you promised me. I belong more to you, Lord, than any scheme in life." My life is yours. Everything is yours. And that total recognition of belonging to the other is the way in which he images who Jesus Christ is—the one who comes in the name of the Father and only does what the Father tells him to do, only announces what the Father has announced.

There's one line here, which is an incredible quotation from Adrienne von Speyr. I like this quotation, and it connects to me to Abraham, although here he's not talking about Abraham. He says, quoting Adrienne von Speyr: "Holiness does not consist in the fact that a man gives everything, but in the fact that the Lord takes everything." And I mean to me those might be Adrienne von Speyr's words, but that's the essence of what Giussani is really trying to get us to see here. Your life doesn't belong to you so much so that your mistakes don't belong to you, your failures don't belong to you, your sin doesn't belong to you. And the question is, can you acknowledge that? Can you face that with honesty and sincerity? Then begins the journey of discovering the "I," discovering oneself as belonging to God. John, do you want to make a comment there? A brief one? We've got a minute and a half.

John Milbank: No, I don't think so. I don't have anything to add really. Thank you very much for those words, Aaron.

Aaron Riches: I've got so many things that I wanted to say to end the conversation. Let me just end by saying one small thing. I'm going to make a quotation from T.S. Eliot, which is not quoted by Father Giussani in the book, but I think is at the essence of what he considers memory to be. There's a line in the *Four Quartets*, where Eliot says, "We had the experience, but we miss the meaning, and the discovery of the meaning returns the experience to us in a completely new valuation of all that we ever were." And this is the use of memory for us. This is the use of the Eucharist, what Father Giussani writes in here in the section on prayer, when he says, "Do this in memory of me" is sort of the summary of the most concrete reality of what prayer is, that this act of memory is to recall the one who comes to us and meets us, and that this one is the one who generates our sense of "I," it is not we.

And so I really want to thank John and Michael. This is for me a beautiful moment of a conspiracy of friendship. All of John's pupils are friends, and we're friends over email, we're friends in person. And it's a sign, really, of the generosity of John himself. And so we're really grateful for that, and I'm super grateful to have been able to have been here and moderated a conversation between Dr. Michael Hanby and Professor John Milbank.

John Milbank: I just wanted to say that I was very grateful for the encounter that I've had and my pupils have had with CL and the legacy of Father Giussani. Thank you.

Michael Hanby: If I could add one last thing. Everything you said is a sign that this is true. And John, it's great to see you. Wish you were here.

Aaron Riches: One last announcement before we go: Father Giussani's *In Search of the Human Face* is on sale at the Human Adventure Book table outside the auditorium. And an important announcement: you are part of the New York Encounter, a place that welcomes everybody. Help us keep this event alive—we invite you to give generously at our donation table outside this auditorium or in a couple of clicks: *newyorkencounter.org*.

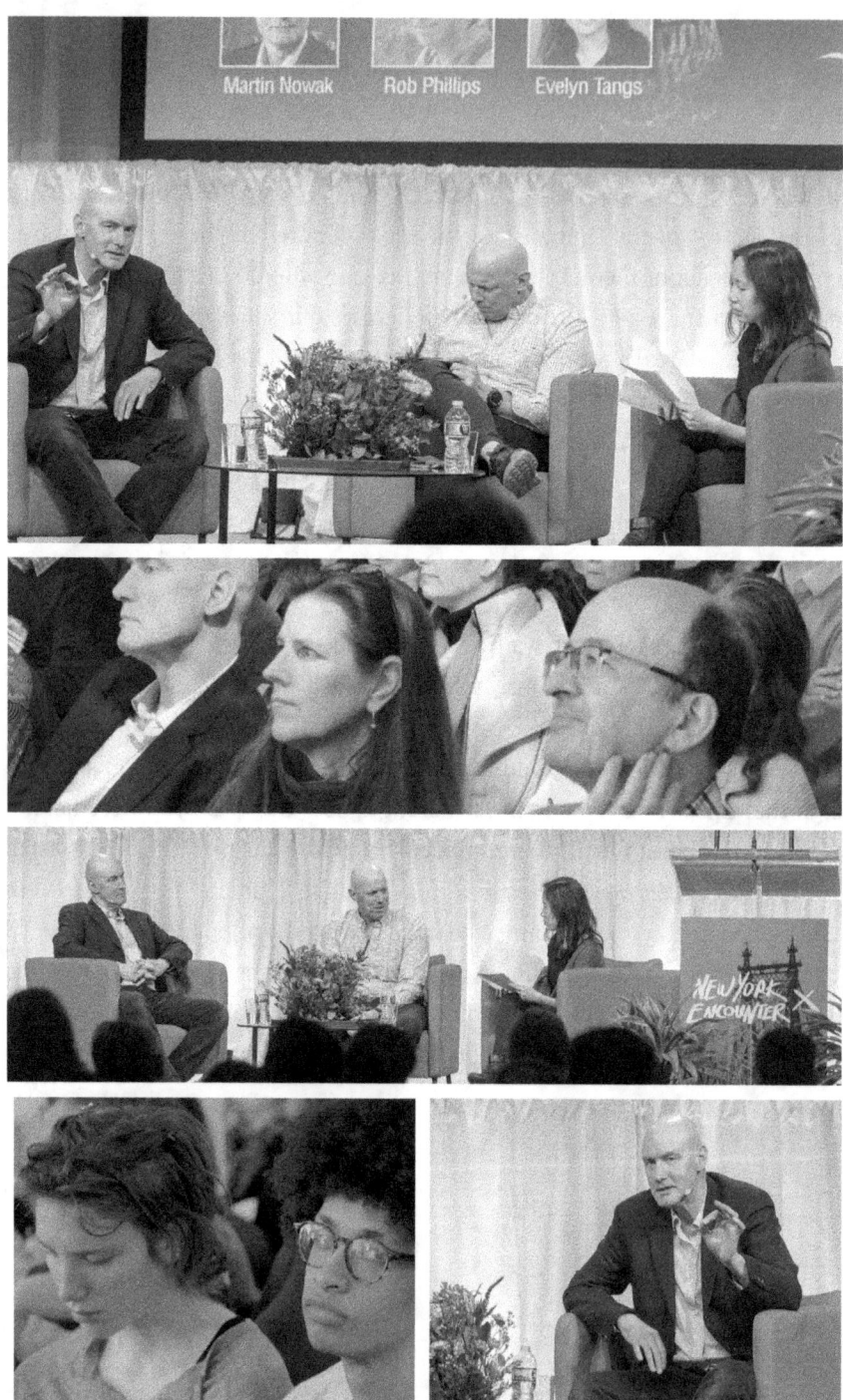

ALL THAT IS NEEDED IS ATTENTION

*Marveling at nature in scientific research with **Martin Nowak**, Professor of Mathematics and Biology, Harvard University, and **Rob Phillips**, Professor of Biophysics, Biology, and Physics at the California Institute of Technology. Moderated by **Evelyn Tang**, Assistant Professor of Physics and Astronomy, Rice University.*

Introduction

It has become increasingly difficult to pay attention to what is in front of us. We have lost the habit of marveling at things and are thus often deprived of a fundamental human experience. The speakers will dialogue on the essential role that attentive observation and wonder play in scientific research and education. They will also address how the practice of science, starting from the experience of awe and curiosity about nature, can evoke existential questions that lead to ultimate meaning.

✠

Evelyn Tang, moderator: Good evening, everyone, and on the Encounter's behalf, welcome both here at the Metropolitan Pavilion and those who are following us online. I am Evelyn Tang, Assistant Professor of Physics and Astronomy at Rice University, and I will moderate this event. Before starting, I would like to thank Spiritual Yearning in Science for sponsoring our conversation. Spiritual Yearning in Science is an initiative directed by Dr. Brandon Vaidyanathan at the Catholic University of America and funded by the John Templeton Foundation.

And now I would like to briefly introduce our speakers. The full bios are on the Encounter website that you can read at leisure. But first of all, Martin Nowak is a professor of mathematics and biology at Harvard. He's a leading researcher in the fields of evolutionary biology and mathematical biology. Martin has established cooperation as the third fundamental principle of evolution, besides mutation and selection. He has published more than 500 papers, many of them in top journals such as Nature and Science, and six books. Martin's most recent books, *Beyond* and *Within*, are poetic explorations of some of the deepest questions that arise at the interface of science, philosophy and religion, and I think we're going to hear more about them tonight.

Rob Phillips is a dear friend and grew up in California in a home filled with books, leading to a love affair with books and reading that continues to this day. He is the Fred and Nancy Morris Professor of Biophysics and Biology at Caltech. Prior to a career full of life and science, Rob spent seven years of travel, self-study, and working as an electrician. Although teaching is often viewed within research universities as a chore, Rob finds teaching to be central in learning about how the world works. He is currently engaged in several projects, one of which, with Ananda Siya, provides a quantitative view of how genes are turned on and off.

I would like to invite them to tell us a bit more about themselves, so please go ahead. Rob, would you like to go ahead and view some slides?

Rob Phillips: Good evening, everyone. Thank you. It's such a huge privilege to be here. I'm a professor in biology and physics at the California Institute of Technology, and I have to say that that's been an amazing stroke of luck. I've spent the last 25 years there, and tonight, my hope for myself in this interesting conversation is to try and give you a little bit of a sense of the spirit that animates spending a life in science. And for me, it really begins very simply with the two words "I wonder." So let's just watch this together.

Video plays

That's great. So if you can go backwards, that would be cool, but it doesn't really matter. So what was my point here? That's a very, in principle, mundane thing, looking at a sea lion swimming around in a school of fish. But for 2000 years, people have been wondering about the starlings over Rome, just for example, how they fly in those weird murmurations, and curiosity really doesn't have to defend itself. It's a beautiful thing that we really still don't understand.

So again, I'm excited for our conversation. I've had a great time listening to many of you already today and meeting you. And I wanted to comment not so much on the content of science, although I'd love to talk about that, but rather about the values.

And some of you might have seen this book long ago. I remember it was on my parents' shelf. I looked at it, it didn't make a very big impression on me, but I do like this idea that maybe some of the most important things we know we learned when we were very young. And the reason I bring this up is that in physics, we have a monthly journal called *Physics Today*, and it has semi-technical journals that help all of us keep up with everything from the smallest to the very largest in the universe, but also has these one-page opinion pieces, and I really like this one. You're not supposed to read what it says, so forget about that. But his title really is inspired by that book that I just showed you, and what he wanted to talk about is, what are the values that one has to actually be a physicist, and I would say a scientist more generally.

And so I thought I would just mention a few that mean a lot to me and that may come up in our conversation. And of course, if I run into you in the hallway, maybe it would be fun to chat about them.

So for sure curiosity. Yesterday, I was at Rockefeller University with a friend of mine. He's—not that I care about such things—but he's a Nobel Prize winner and a postdoc, but I'm serious about that. I don't care very much, and I don't think he does either, but he was telling me about his postdoc, and he said, "This guy is so amazing because he's childlike in his curiosity," and both of us agreed that that sort of innocence, the childlike innocence, is something that actually is often lost. And in many ways the most fun in science is not losing that openness. It's hard to learn things if you've already made up your mind. And so when we're looking at the natural world, for example, the sea lion, there's all sorts of possible explanations of things, and we don't know, a priori, what they are, which leads to, "I don't know."

There's a sort of technical thing that we often use in science, which is called a null hypothesis. And for me, the most useful null hypothesis is, "I don't know." Love is the truth wherever it may lead. Gratitude, you don't know other people's narratives, not being opinionful. This one's very important to me. I learned it from Robert Nozick in his book *The Examined Life*. I don't have to have an opinion about everything. And it's liberating, I would say. And that's helpful in science, the mystery of the world that's already present in a simple, mundane thing, like a sea lion swimming in a school of fish. Amazement that the human mind has achieved what it has in terms of uncovering a little bit of the mystery of the world around us in a way that, in general, we agree on implicitly, if not explicitly.

And for me, also respect for the achievements of the past. You know, one of the things that came up and is shown in that video, but I very much appreciate, I'm very dedicated to celebrating Archimedes. I know that Martin's going to talk about mathematics as well. He and I share this great love of the tradition of mathematics. I'll come to that in a moment, not taking things for granted. Knowledge is hard. Be careful—improving upon silence is hard. And instead of "Here's what I know," instead saying, "Here's the way I'm thinking about it."

So in my teaching, one of the things that's been my greatest privilege is trying to take students out into the world. I have a huge responsibility when I meet 20-year-olds, 18-year-olds at Caltech. And so I've led on the order of 20 field trips to the Galapagos, to Indonesia, to New Zealand. And often we spend 20 to 40 minutes a day in silence, every one of us with one of these little green notebooks, which is waterproof, and we basically either draw the rocks or draw the animals or write questions that start with the words, "I wonder."

So this one may be perhaps weird for this audience, but most of the way we've been communicating with each other today has been with words, and that's cool, but I just wanted to put a plug in for the idea that maybe it's interesting to communicate about the world using mathematics and numbers, and it's really actually very powerful. And also, I know Martin will mention this, or I think he will, it's also, in a certain sense, very spiritual, at least for me.

So my final thought is just to say that in Paris, at the ESPCI, which is a scientific institution where Pierre and Marie Curie worked and where they discovered radium, if you look on this wall, you'll see this line from *Miguel Mañara*. I don't remember how to pronounce his name. It says to question and doubt. It says true science teaches, above all, to doubt. So for me, that's really the essence of things. So that's all I got. So I'm looking forward to the discussion.

Martin Nowak: Oh, wow. It's a great honor and joy for me to be here. I have been at the New York Encounter once before, and it's great to be back.

Yes, that's right, that's almost—yes, that's right. So here we are. "All that is needed is attention." That's the topic of our little conversation here. And I was very, very moved by the video that is on the homepage of the New York Encounter 2025, and so I also use it in my talk several times.

All that is needed is attention. So we're living in the following world where many people think that science is a distraction from spirituality. Science is almost something that is at odds with believing in God. And I want to change this. I want to change this in the opposite view, because I think if we pay attention to what science really says, it leads us to God. And that's the message of my talk: science leads us to God.

So when we pay attention, we have to ask, like a child—Rob mentioned a child-like approach—like a child, what are the most important things that actually science puts as landmarks out there. What are the three things that really happened? And the one thing is the origin of the universe. The second thing is the origin of life, and the third thing is the origin of language, of human language. And what do these events give us? The universe gives us physics. This is really the beginning of a physics that is unfolding. Stars are being produced. They make chemical elements. So that gives us physics and chemistry, the origin of life gives us biology.

What does language give us? The first thing that language gives us is prayer, because as soon as humans had language, they were spiritual beings. The findings in the Chauvet cave and in other places are expressions of a kind of spirituality. So I would argue, as soon as humans have language, you talk about spirituality, about God; as soon as humans have language, you discover the world of ideas, and here I mean Platonic ideas, forms. You have poetry, you have philosophy, you have the discovery of mathematics. You have the discovery of science, of technology, engineering and medicine. All that matters very, very deeply to us is a derivative of language.

And why is language as big as the origin of life itself? Because it gives rise to a new way of evolution, because we have evolution no longer in the genetic realm. We have it also in the cognitive, linguistic realm.

This is the time scale if we want to add a few more other events. So when did it happen? Big Bang, 13.8 billion years ago. Sun, 4.6 billion years ago. Physicists always know things very, very well. And my critics criticized me for worshiping physics, but I asked, "What is there not to worship?"

And in biology, things are sort of more complicated. So origin of life, we are maybe on Earth, we don't really know, but what we all agree is that bacteria are here, where they are 3.5 billion years ago. The higher cells with organelles, 1.8 billion years ago, and all the while until 600 million years ago, if you come to Earth, you see no sign of life without a microscope. So this was all microscopic life, things that you see with the naked eye comes into existence 600 million years ago. This is the complex multicellularity.

And then the last big thing, what is the most interesting thing that happened in the last 600 million years? That is the arrival of human language, because it gives rise to a new way of evolution.

So the forces of physics we can conclude, and evolution leads to living beings that raise their voices in praise of God, that discover underlying unchanging truth. And here I'm stating a fact. This is a scientific fact: physics and evolution has led to people who recognize spirituality.

What is it that evolves? Ernst Mayr, a Harvard biologist, pointed this out that loosely speaking, we talk about evolution of genes and so, but what really evolves is the population. So the carrier of the evolutionary process is the population. The two classic ingredients of evolution recognized by Darwin—even though not properly understood—is mutation and selection. So Darwinian evolution is based on mutation and selection. Selection means that different types grow at different rates.

And to this, my work over the last 20 years and the work of many others, has really added cooperation as a fundamental additional principle of evolution. And cooperation means that individuals work together so well that they form a higher level of organization. Cooperation, in my mind, is the master architect of the evolutionary process. Whenever something amazing happens in evolution, like the direction of life itself, or the first cells or human language, cooperation needs to be involved. Cooperation is that which leads to human language. So I call it the master architect of the evolutionary process.

Cooperation means helping others. And here we have three examples of what helping others means. The one is 3 billion years old. This is cyanobacteria. And every so often, a cell dies in order to feed the others with nitrogen. So this is the ultimate sacrifice. The cell dies so others can live.

Social insects, as Wilson was mentioned this afternoon, these individuals don't reproduce. They help another individual to reproduce, 125 million years ago.

This is Vincent Van Gogh's painting of the Good Samaritan, and we all know what that is. That is cooperation among humans.

One nice element of this analysis that winning strategies of cooperation are generous, hopeful and forgiving. This is based on a game theoretic analysis of how to win. Those strategies that succeed, they know how to be generous, they know how to be hopeful, and they know how to forgive. So therefore, evolution is not only competition. It's also cooperation. It was cooperation from the beginning, the great discoveries of evolution are impossible without cooperation. And finally, cooperation is a preparation for altruism, for agape and for love. This is why it is okay now to talk of humans or to ask of humans to actually like each other, because without cooperation, we would have been the product of just some fight out there.

Nevertheless, we are now at this stage where the survival of intelligent life on Earth is actually in a critical situation, in my opinion. So for the survival of the human species, we need more than what we have now. We need global cooperation, and we need cooperation with future generations, and right now, we are actually doing exactly the opposite. We don't cooperate on a global scale, and we don't cooperate in order to leave a better world to the next generation.

What we need is a science of love. And "Science of Love" is actually a term that is coined by one of my favorite saints, and you will encounter her at the very end. We need a science of love, a pandemic of goodness and the return to God. We need attention in order to solve this problem of global cooperation. And here begins a new life with this attention.

So if science makes you aware of that which matters, the encounter with a great love gives us a glimpse of a mysterious presence, the ultimate beauty and love, whom we have always expected, but never met. And this kind of encounter led me to write these books.

For many years, I wanted to write books that bring together science and religion, science and God, but I didn't really find the voice. And then suddenly the voice that was in me was the idea that I let a female Divine Presence talk about it while I'm only listening.

So the encounter with a great love has the power to transform the world. And this first book *Beyond* is really a meditation on God and love. It's a dialog between a male Faustian voice and a mysterious female presence, an unnamed Beatrice—that was actually written by one of the people who commented on the book—who becomes his guide to leave the cave of shadows.

What *Beyond* wants to say is that beyond this world of change is an unchanging reality. And this unchanging reality is, for example, represented in mathematics or in truth, but also in love and in God. In order to see this, all that is needed is attention.

And just in the last few days, I published another book, and this is called *Within*. And here the idea is really that God is waiting for us within, as our teacher, as the love of our life, as a lover and beloved. And if you have this view that you realize from every pair of eyes that is looking at you, it is God that is looking at you. And you also realize that the purpose of human life is to find God by love.

And this book is completely inspired and devoted by one of the greatest saints that lived in the last 500 years. And this is her, and one of my favorite quotes of her is "In the heart of the church, my mother, I will be love, and thus I will be all things as my desire finds its direction." Thank you very much.

Evelyn Tang: Wonderful. I think we're very curious about how your own personal journey and experiences have shaped, you know, all of this beautiful fruits that you've been telling us about. So we're curious about how your scientific questions and ideas arise, and in particular, why do you believe that mathematics and harmonious principles govern nature? So Rob, you spoke about science and this quest, this constant doubting, this constant search for truth. This is an exhausting quest. Why did you devote your life to it? Or Martin, that you believe that mathematics and cooperation governs nature. These seem like audacious claims and audacious quests, given how messy nature is. Why are we looking for these principles and these ideas?

Rob Phillips: Yeah, well, maybe I'll take a crack at both of those. So as far as how, you know, I think there's no one answer, obviously, and everybody's different. But in my case, I would say there's maybe four different kinds of things.

So one is amazement. So I want all of you to imagine the following crazy experiment. I have my hand, my arms out. You cut off this arm. This arm grows shorter. This arm starts to grow. When they're the same length, they grow back out. So that sounds crazy, but that's exactly what you will observe in a microscopic organism with a microscope called Stentor coeruleus. And you know, that's enough. It's so interesting and so unusual that that's enough to say is that worth spending five years of a graduate student's life on?

Dissatisfaction? You know, that's another example. No. But seriously, it's a huge responsibility. When a 20-year-old comes to you and says, "I want to do a PhD," you're asking them to spend five or six years of their life working on something. So I feel like you have to take that seriously. And I'm telling you, I think that fascinating question is worth it.

I would say dissatisfaction, you know, the fact that there are things we should understand that we don't. So that's a big one for me. And then where questions come from is learning and teaching. I think that that's, you know, there's no distinction between teaching and research for me.

Just a quick note before Martin goes on, the subject of the audacious notion of principles. I think evidence forces it on us. You know, Caltech sent out an email a few years ago saying, "Show up at the athletic field at such and such time, because there's going to be a transit of Venus." There were 10 micro-telescopes set up, and we went over there as a family, and sure enough, Venus appeared. It crossed the sun and it left. You know, an eclipse is, you know, it's not controversial. It's evidence of these audacious principles, I guess is what I would say, because the mathematics works.

Martin Nowak: It's interesting to note that both Plato and Aristotle held mathematical knowledge in high regard. They held mathematical knowledge higher than things that you know based on experiences, but they did not know something that is very important. They did not realize that mathematics was the language of nature, ultimately, because at this time, this was not established. So it was kind of an additional trick that was used by somebody to do certain things. But it was not realized as the language of physics, and definitely not as biology.

It was Johannes Kepler who was the first person to believe in a physical interpretation, the physical reality of a mathematical calculation. And I would also say Galilei. And so therefore physics developed very strongly with this connection with mathematics. But biology didn't have this. So at that time it was understood, the heavens were perfect and the heavens could be described mathematically—the planets—but the earth was so messy that mathematics doesn't work here and is not sort of real.

Much later came this idea that biology is also subject to mathematical analysis, and this is what has fascinated me throughout my life, the mathematics of biology. And I would argue we have reached a stage now where in biology we know things if we know them mathematically, we understand evolutionary aspects if we can understand them mathematically.

Evelyn Tang: I think we would all agree, given that we are trying to use mathematics, all three of us, to study biology.

Let's go to the theme, the provoking theme of our panel itself, which is "all that is needed is attention." This is a very strong claim. How do you feel about it? Do you agree with it? And even better, could you share an example from your own experience where attention or wonder allowed you to discover something new?

And I think related to this is, you know, Rob already said that in research and teaching to him that's connected. So if attention is important to you, does this shape your teaching and how we encourage our students to think and consider today?

In our panels today, we have been discussing so much about the role of technology and how that impacts the way that students, you know, don't look up as much as they did, or don't speak to each other as much as we did. How do we inculcate or foster this attention? Or, relatedly, what has been the role of teachers in our own lives?

Martin Nowak: I would take it in the following way, that sometimes we are blindly accepting scientific statements and in order to really interpret them, we need attention. So I give you, I think, two examples.

One example is the scientific statement that was made: "Science has shown the universe exists for no reason and has no purpose." And so now you have to pay attention what is being said here actually, to really understand whether you agree with this or not.

So first of all, the statement itself assumes that the person who said it has a method to distinguish between a universe that has a purpose and the universe that doesn't have a purpose, and has a method to distinguish between a universe that exists for a reason and the universe that exists for no reason, and science somehow has—and this is not true if you think about it. So science does precisely not show that. So this is a philosophical statement, if you want to say this, but science doesn't do this.

Something else, which I find very interesting. Sometimes there was a strong insistence that evolution is taught in the following way: evolution is an unguided process. So when you talk about evolution, you have to say it, it's an unguided process. So if I hear this sentence, I have to ask, unguided by what? So you are already an atheist, you know. So why do you say it's an unguided process? Do you also say gravity is an unguided process?

So I think we need attention when we want to interpret science properly, to give us a broader world view, and to tell us who we are.

Rob Phillips: Maybe I'll tell a story that happened a couple months ago on a United flight. I'm excited. I already got my flight for tomorrow. I know my seat. I have a right hand window seat on a 787, and I was flying back from Europe, and for a great reason, the captain, a woman on United, she came back to greet all the people in business class, and I said, "I'm really excited about Greenland today." And you all might not believe this, but I'm telling you the truth. In the middle of the flight, the captain came back to wake me up because she said it was one of the greatest days she's ever seen.

The reason I bring this up is I'm always very puzzled. I find your question in a way puzzling, which is, I don't understand how people don't pay attention. Just to give you an example, why are all the windows closed when you're flying over Greenland? But seriously, you know, like mine's open, and I was sitting there, and a person next to me called the flight attendant and I could hear her. She said, "Could you tell that guy that I'm watching a movie and he's got the window up." And I said, and she rotated by 180 degrees and told me that. And I said, "Could you tell her that I'm flying in an aluminum tube at roughly the speed of sound, that Greenland is right down there. And if you ask somebody 300 years ago, 'Would you like to see Greenland from the sky?' they probably say yes."

So that's what I try. Wow, thank you. Okay, well, so I don't know. I mean, honestly, I feel really out of place, because kids notice things, and I just feel like maybe, here's the way I would say it is, I think that we don't take ourselves seriously. That's my honest answer to you about the question of attention, which is, if you have a thought, like in science, if you have a thought and you take it seriously, you just gave yourself maybe five years' work, right? So if you take it seriously, you've got to follow it. You can't just say like that, you have to follow it. So that's a formal way to have attention, I guess. So I trust that process a ton, not only in science, but in life, like if I pay attention, I feel it pays off anyway. That's very personal. It's subjective. It's not anything anyone else might share. But that's my take on it.

Evelyn Tang: Yeah, I think that no, the reason why this panel here exists, and we're putting this idea of attention and science together is precisely because I think in science, the way in which we pay attention is particularly deep. It can go particularly focused.

I'm going to read a quote by Simone Weil where she wrote that

"Attention consists of suspending our thoughts, leaving it detached, empty and ready to be penetrated by the objects. It means holding in our minds within reach of this thought, but on a lower level and not in contact with it, the diverse knowledge we have acquired, which we are forced to make use of."

So it's a very complex process where you pay attention to something, but you also relate it with lots of other things. We see Greenland, but we also think about now, I'm seeing it from a distance, or I think of a statement, and I'm not just taking the statement at face value, but I'm interrogating it with the different methods that I have of how to understand the statement. And this is particular focus that I think that you know, we'd love to hear you guys speak to, but what that journey has been is very particular and specific, and so also about your experiences and how this might shape your teaching.

Rob Phillips: An experiment is actually a way of paying attention. So check this out. So you know, I just dropped something, and all of us have experienced that at one time or another. But Galileo, you know, he spent years on that. He had to figure out how to slow down time by using an inclined plane. You know, there's many Italians here, and I love that. So I just led a tour, actually, of Italy to go to Galileo's home in Florence, and we went to see Enrico Fermi. So anyway, an experiment, I mean, I don't know if you've thought of it that way, but an experiment is a way of paying attention. That's what an experiment is. It's a formalization of attention, right? I mean, do you buy that?

Evelyn Tang: I mean, it's a repeated, constant probing of what's going on. Fantastic. You know, Martin, I think you've been, you know, you told us about how your ideas and mathematics are, perhaps, you know, you tell your students about what you think about mathematics. And this is challenging because it's not conventional. So we'd love to, and Rob, you told us about how you bring our students to the Galapagos. So we'd love to hear about how also your ideas, about paying attention, about the material and immaterial are brought into your teaching. Or conversely, you know what has been the role of teachers in your lives?

Martin Nowak: So the role of teachers in the life of a scientist is profound. I was very, very fortunate that my PhD advisor, Karl Sigmund, in Vienna, stayed my lifelong friend. And the first thing that I always do when I go back to Vienna is I walk with him in the forest, and we have the conversations—the same kind of conversations we had when I was his PhD student. We've continued to work for many, many years. And my mentor in Oxford was Robert May. He was president of the Royal Society later. But my mentor in this science-religion field was Sarah Coakley. She is an ordained priest in the Church of England, but she always taught me Catholic philosophy, I'm glad to say. So this is what I learned from her.

But here is another element that I think—some of the greatest moments where I learned something was from my own students, from the students in class, from the PhD students, from the postdocs, when they gave me answers and surprising insights that really moved me. So I think as a scientist, you are always a learner, and even if you teach a class, you are actually the learner, and you benefit greatly from the questions of the students and from the interactions with the students.

Rob Phillips: Yeah. So first of all, in terms of shaping teaching, I guess I just feel like the constant emphasis on performance metrics really deprives us of what I think of—I mean, this is kind of obnoxious, but I think of there's a Hippocratic oath for teaching, which is, you shouldn't kill souls. I don't, I don't mean that in the, you know, the usual way. But like Evelyn and I had an amazing experience, which was, we went up to the 100-inch telescope on Mount Wilson. If you fly to LA, if you get a right-hand window seat, you will be able to see where the fire is burned. But on the top, you'll be able to see the 100-inch telescope where Edwin Hubble discovered the expanding universe. And I've taken 200 students and faculty members. You and I went there together. It's kind of mind-blowing to do that.

So I guess what I would say about, how does paying attention focus my own teaching—I don't really care about teaching Fourier transforms and PDEs and all these formal things. I care about, can people start sentences with the two words "I wonder."

As far as teachers for me in particular, I feel that we failed each other. So I left high school after 11th grade, I really resented my high school experience, which is where I came to my view on the Hippocratic Oath of teaching. And so I think at least for my teens and something, you know, my greatest teachers were weird people in books like Euclid and Archimedes and things like that. But I agree with Martin, you know, you learn from your students. That's the beauty of this enterprise of science. You know, we're all essentially equally ignorant.

The thing about the way I would represent grad school, and I don't know if this is true in the fields that we've heard people from today, but in science, it's a kind of learning about the unknown. You're not learning about the known, you're learning about the unknown, and nobody knows the answer. If somebody knows the answer, you're not working on the right problem.

Martin Nowak: That's exactly right. This is this very beautiful experience of a scientist—is that you always stand before the unknown. And in some sense, what is known is almost boring, and so you don't even want to look too much at what is known. You constantly, every day, every morning you get up, you stand before the unknown, and the unknown is always in front of you. And science will never be done, and mathematics will never be done. And that's the beauty of it. And you have to ask yourself, why is this? Why will mathematics never be done? Why will science never be done? And the priest gave me the answer: because God is an infinite being, and we will never understand an infinite being.

Evelyn Tang: So you both have extremely interesting stories and life paths and also interests, and we'd love to hear how all of this has made you the scientists and mathematicians that you are. So besides reading scientific books and articles, do you read other things or spend time with friends and family? Basically, I'm curious about what helps you in your research, and if there is a relation with your personal pursuits.

Rob Phillips: You want to go first? Okay, sure. So first of all, I really feel very strongly about this, the subject of this particular session, which is that one has to formalize paying attention, you know, that asking a question, taking it seriously, and then trying to figure out, how am I going to actually make falsifiable progress on it? You know, there's a lot of hot air.

I guess I would say, I think reading—you know, I love the video at the beginning, because I think that it's true that we don't respect, we don't respect, somehow, the past. And I really can't tell you how much I see that in 18-year-olds. They don't know that much about the history of science or the history of things more generally. And so it's pretty awesome to be able to read, I don't know, whatever—Moby Dick, but also the latest romance novel. I think it's all great.

And so you were asking about friends and family. I don't really acknowledge—I just feel like I'm a spoiled person that gets paid to goof around.

Evelyn Tang: Rob, regarding, you know, friends and family. I suppose we met because you were bringing together a group of people that you want to build community with. So clearly, you know, friends and community is important to you for sure. And you know, Martin, I've, you know, I met some of your collaborators. I told you before I even met you. So I know also that you have a strong level of collaborators who you're very close with. And so clearly this is something that's also important in your journeys.

Rob Phillips: Actually, maybe this is interesting. Some people have a philosophy like they will go out into the world to find that collaborator, that scientist that will be most helpful for their enterprise, and I kind of don't share that, because if that person's not fun to interact with, then I'm not going to go hang out with them. So what can I tell you?

Martin Nowak: I also completely agree that I see science very much as a collaborative enterprise, and you absolutely need to work together with people who are your friends. Where the friends come from—for me, great moments of inspiration were when I first came to university, and in physics class, the professor performed an experiment in front of the class, and then he says, "In order to understand the experiment, we have to calculate." So this was the first time that I realized mathematics was not just there to give homeworks to high school kids, but it's actually to understand something. And that fascination then drove me to become—I wanted to become a theoretician, somebody who uses mathematics to describe first chemistry and then biology.

And in this endeavor between science and religion, there were many moments—when I came to Harvard, I first met Sarah Coakley, and she was a professor at Divinity School, and I realized from her I could learn how to speak what I wanted to say about science and God, because at that time, I wasn't able to do that. That's cool.

Then came a moment when I was deeply fascinated, and I still am, by the *Bhagavad Gita*. So the *Bhagavad Gita*—Gandhi calls it the gospel of selflessness. And in the *Bhagavad Gita*, we are asked to think of the sufferings of others as our own, to see the same God in every other person. The *Bhagavad Gita* is a call for selfless action. You are asked to act in the world selflessly, but you shouldn't be attached to the outcomes of the action. So the *Bhagavad Gita* was a huge spiritual inspiration for me, and it is mentioned in *Beyond*.

After that, I read the *Katha Upanishad*, and the *Katha Upanishad* describes the soul as fusing with God. Then I asked Sarah Coakley again, "Do we have the same in Christianity?" And she says, "It is not really the standard vision, but I should read Teresa of Ávila." And so then I read Teresa of Ávila, *The Interior Castle*, and I was deeply moved. And for the first time, I got a glimpse of what it takes to actually love your enemies, and how she was able to do that. Something has to happen in your life if you want to love your enemies.

I was done with Teresa of Ávila, and I said, "All my life I knew there was this big Teresa and the little Teresa. And I have never, ever bothered to read anything about the little Teresa. Now I want to find out about the little Teresa." And then I started to read, and I was captivated and mesmerized beyond description, and my life changed. And then I had this feeling she was always present in my life, but I was not worthy yet to know her directly. And at that moment, the revelation came. She revealed herself to me, as she has to hundreds of thousands of other people before me, because this is really her role. She said, "My life begins after my death. I will not just be in heaven. I will tirelessly work to bring souls to God."

Evelyn Tang: That was her mission, in a sense. That's beautiful. I am so struck by how the both of you have been reiterating this idea that there is this mystery, that even the more we know, the more we don't know. That there's so much that you would say we don't know, and then we have to ask. And that is always this infinite that's continuing, you know? And Einstein said as well, that the most beautiful thing we can experience is the mysterious. It is the source of all true arts and science. So this seems to be a theme, something that is urging us on, that's making us look, and so, you know, I'm curious, does being in front of nature and its laws that you find, that you discover, does it evoke more profound existential questions than you? And where are these questions leading you?

Rob Phillips: Yeah, I actually should have said, when I was showing the video of the sea lion, that there was—I think it's apocryphal, because I tried to trace this quote, unquote remark from Einstein, where he said, you have two options. You can either treat everything as mysterious or nothing. And I really just find that the former is way better in every regard. You know, it's more useful, it makes you happier, I think, to view something as simple as a view out an airplane over Greenland, or just encountering all of you on the stage, as kind of mysterious.

Of course, for me—I can't speak for anyone else, but of course, it elicits other questions, and I very much appreciate what Martin was saying about mathematics, because that's been one of the great things in my life, is the realization that by pure thought, I could write down an equation that could tell me how old the Galapagos are. You know, like, I know that there's such an equation. I didn't look it up in any book. I just figured out what it was and wrote it down, and I found out, yeah, that works.

But at the same time, as we heard this morning in some of the other talks, that may not be helpful when faced with a very human question, you know, like, how to be a parent, let's keep it simple. Anybody that's a parent in the room, I imagine, has understood that feeling. You know, you think you have some concept of what it means to be a parent, and then you get a curveball, and most of us are not good at hitting curveballs, is what I've seen. So, yeah, it elicits all sorts of questions.

And since there's so many Italians here, I've already said this to a few of you, there's an Italian author, Dino Buzzati—I'm not sure I pronounced his name correctly. And my all-time favorite short story of all time is by him, and I translated it from French to English for my dad, because it didn't exist in English, while he was in the process of dying from cancer. And it's not something I would normally be attached to. It's very much relevant to all of you, in the sense that if you have a background of Catholicism, that will mean the world to you, but it's called *Humility*, and I feel like that's part of this issue about about the mystery, like it's very easy to march around in this world, acting like you've got the bull by the horns, but in science, nor in life, in my opinion, do any of us have the bull by the horns.

Martin Nowak: It's very difficult to—this is already such a complete description, but I think one quote attributed to Einstein is that his success was based on the fact that he never stopped asking the questions that only a child would ask. Coming back to that—something else attributed to him, which I like even more, is actually, "If I could explain what I was doing, it wouldn't be research." And this is this sentence I always want to use in my grant writing.

And I think it's right that nature is immensely beautiful. And as a scientist, you find nature mysterious, and you ask yourself certain questions and you want to give explanations. So here's another anecdote from the history of science. Johannes Kepler is very much associated with these three laws of Kepler, but these three laws of Kepler, they were basically discovered by Newton. Newton went through all of Kepler's works and then found these three things out there and realized this is what he can explain.

This is great. Kepler himself never considered this his main contributions at all. So the first Kepler law is that the planets go on ellipses. He considered it an embarrassment. This was not a discovery. This cannot really be true because it wasn't beautiful enough. And for the second law, he derived an approximation, which he then later proved to be false. Then he forgot about that, and all his life, he used the false approximation for the second law. The third law was hidden in a book of 800 pages on the harmony of the spheres.

So why did Kepler not pay attention to these first three Kepler laws? Because when he was 25 years old, he had already discovered the most beautiful thing that is out there. He had discovered why there are six planets and why they have the relative distance from each other. This needed to be explained at that time. So at that time, the solar system had six planets and they had a certain distance—that distance could be measured. And Kepler understood why, and this is how he did it.

He at first used two-dimensional models of mathematics to have polygons and circles, so like a triangle and then a circle around it, then maybe a square and a circle around it, and he tried to fit it in some sense. And whatever he did, it didn't work. And then he realized, "I'm stupid. The universe is not two-dimensional. It's three-dimensional. So I will do the same thing in three dimensions."

So in three dimensions, what are my solids? The platonic solids. So there are only five platonic solids in three dimensions. So he has five platonic solids, six spheres inside and outside. He arranges them a little bit and has the right distances. At that moment, he realizes this is how God created the solar system. And he persuaded the Emperor to build that model in silver. So for him, that was the biggest contribution, not quite right, but very beautiful.

Rob Phillips: Yeah. But, I mean, I think I love that, and I agree with it, and we can just keep going, you know, like Lamarck had his ideas about evolution and so on, and I think that there's something for all of us to learn, first of all, like philosophically about humility, but it also has to do with how hard it is to figure stuff out, and it takes hundreds of years. So I don't know, I personally find when I'm walking around and I run into all the answer-havers—maybe you've got the platonic solids arranged to give me the distances of the planets.

Evelyn Tang: Unfortunately, our time is coming to a close. I would like to remind all of you that at 7pm, so right after this event, Martin will be available to sign his new books *Beyond* and *Within* at the Human Adventure book table right outside the auditorium. And I want to give one important announcement before closing this event: this Encounter is a little big miracle in the heart of New York City. It is a place for all those who seek belonging. So we invite you to give generously at our donation table outside this auditorium, or in a couple of clicks at *www.newyorkencounter. org/donate*. And now please thank me, and please join me in thanking our speakers.

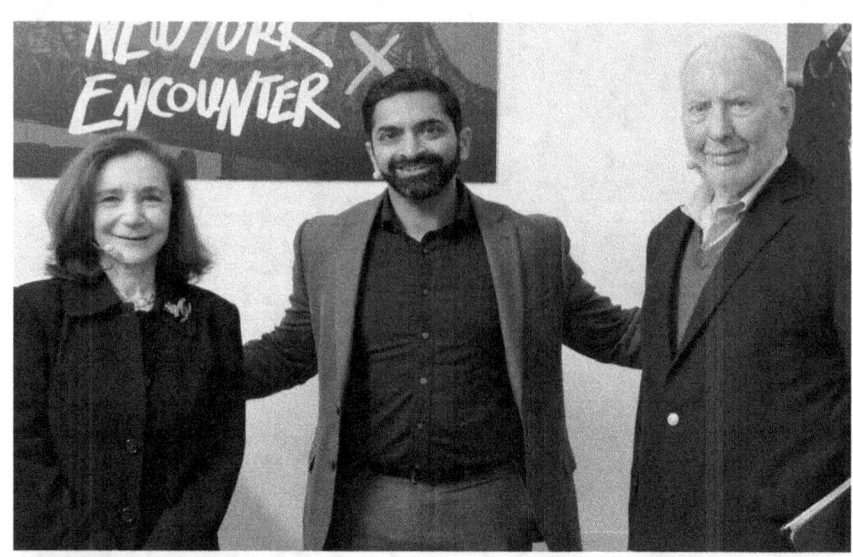

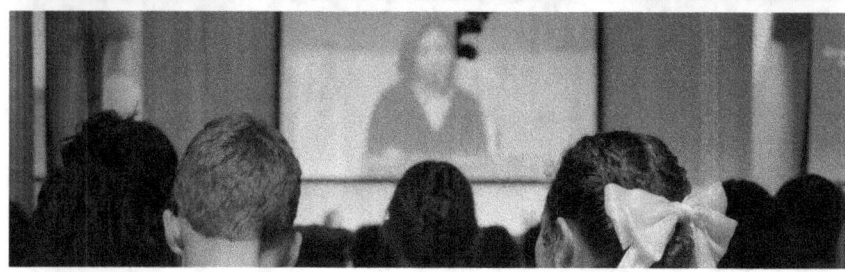

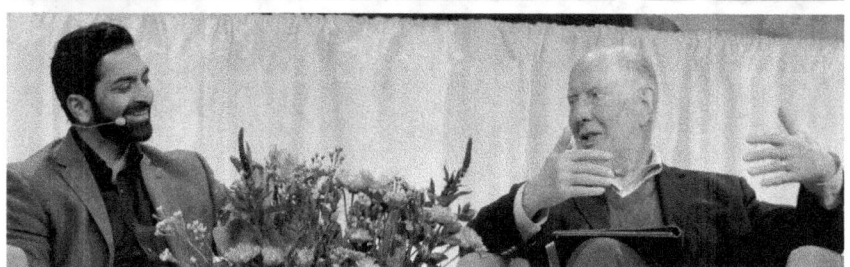

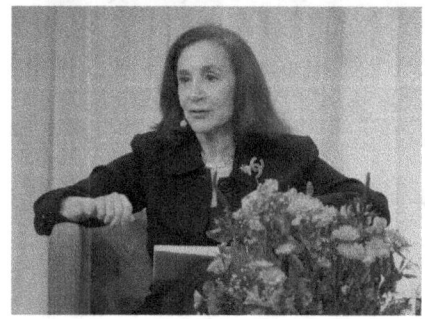
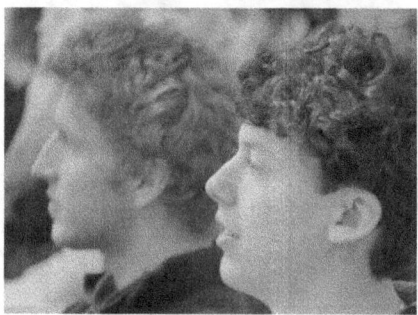

A FEELING OF PRECARIOUSNESS

*A conversation on loneliness and malaise in today's society with **Robert Putnam**, Professor of Public Policy, Harvard University, and **Sherry Turkle**, Professor of the Social Studies of Science and Technology, Massachusetts Institute of Technolog. Moderated by **Brandon Vaidyanathan**, Professor of Sociology, The Catholic University of America*

Introduction

There is no doubt that loneliness and a widespread malaise characterize the lives of young and not-so-young generations. The speakers have dedicated their professional careers to studying societal changes and will look at the root causes of this unease. They will also discuss the impact of social media on human identity and relationships and reflect on ways to address them.

✠

Brandon Vaidyanathan, moderator: Good morning, everyone. On behalf of the New York Encounter, I want to welcome everybody here, those of us joining us in person, in the flesh at the Metropolitan Pavilion, and also those of us joining us online. I'm Brandon Vaidyanathan, a professor of sociology at the Catholic University of America, and I will moderate this conversation. Before we begin, I want to thank Somos for generously sponsoring this panel, and I invite Ms. Riquelmy Lamour, Director of Behavioral Health and Social Work at Somos, to share a few words about what Somos does and its mental health impact.

Riquelmy Lamour: Oh, hello. It's an honor to be here today right before such an important conversation on loneliness and malaise. I know I'm not the main event here. Think of me as your commercial break or that ad you can't skip before the video. But trust me, what I'm about to share connects directly to the discussion ahead.

My name is Riquelmy Lamour. I'm the Director of Behavioral Health at Somos Community Care. You all have these little blue pamphlets on your chair. I am here to tell you about this organization, an organization that is not only transforming healthcare, but actively addressing the very crisis of disconnection that Professor Putnam and Dr. Turkle are here to discuss today. At Somos, we believe that health is not just about medicine, it's about connection. We're a physician-led network dedicated to improving healthcare in some of the most underserved communities in New York City, and we know that you can't separate physical health from mental health, because anyone who's ever had a doctor's appointment before their morning coffee knows that mental health is seriously important, right?

In all seriousness, we see firsthand how social isolation, financial struggles, and systemic barriers make mental health challenges hard. However, we also see how human connection restores them. That's why at Somos we integrate behavioral health into the primary care level, because people are more likely to seek help when it's accessible, familiar and stigma-free. Through programs like our impact model, we provide real-time mental health interventions right at the doctor's office. It's like a one-stop shop, except you're not getting snacks and soda. You're getting support, healing, and connection.

I was recently moved by a talk that I watched on YouTube from last year's SEEKS conference by Dr. Matthew Brenninger, a clinical psychologist. He shared this story about a five-year-old boy in therapy who had been removed from an unsafe and extremely abusive home. This little guy came into therapy, and he was furious. He had just been separated from his family. He was flipping chairs. He was screaming, he was cursing. He was threatening to hurt himself and the doctor. Now, if you've ever been around a five-year-old, you know they can be dramatic, right? But this was different. He was in survival mode, overwhelmed by fear and pain, and what did the therapist do? He didn't yell. He didn't scold. Instead, he simply held him gently but firmly. And the little boy's body softened, his breathing slowed, and he just collapsed in this doctor's arms, crying and finally letting go and finding rest. Why is this important? At this moment, he didn't need words. He needed presence. He needed to know he was safe.

This story resonated with me, because in many ways, this is what we seek to do at Somos, not just offer services, but restore connection. Our work isn't just about treating symptoms, it's about seeing people, standing with them in their suffering, and saying, "You are not alone. We are here." We live in a time when loneliness has become an epidemic. And honestly, that's kind of wild, right? Because on your birthday, you can get 1000 Happy Birthday messages on Facebook, but still eat that cake alone. The reality is that despite technology, more people than ever feel unseen, unheard and disconnected. But what if the solution wasn't complicated? What if it was as simple as showing up, listening and holding space for someone else?

This is the heart of our work at Somos. We train healthcare providers in trauma-informed care. We host community mental health events, wellness workshops, and we bring mental health into the community, into the street. And this is why this is so important. This discussion today, loneliness and malaise aren't just social issues. They are public health crises. They affect our well-being, our communities and our collective future. So as we move into this conversation, I invite you to reflect on this. What if we built a world where no one had to fight their battles alone, where every person, whether at a doctor's office or at a school or a moment in crisis, knew that someone saw them, valued them and would walk with them toward healing? At Somos, this is our vision, and we hope it can be yours too. Thank you so much.

Brandon Vaidyanathan: Thank you, Riquelmy. Today we're going to talk about loneliness and social isolation, and these are issues that have profound implications for our personal well-being and our collective lives together. To put this crisis in perspective, as Riquelmy said, the US Surgeon General has recently declared loneliness a public health epidemic, equating its health risks to smoking 15 cigarettes a day, which I know for some of you is breakfast, but still... yeah, you all should stop.

About 30% of Americans report feeling lonely at least once a week.

Thirty percent of young adults report feeling lonely several times a week. Social media use is linked to rising rates of anxiety and depression among adolescents. So what has brought us to this point today, and what do we do about it? We are honored to be joined by two incredibly distinguished scholars to help us make sense of our crisis and how to move forward.

Dr. Sherry Turkle is the Abby Rockefeller Mauzé Professor of the Social Studies of Science and Technology in the Program in Science, Technology and Society at MIT, and the founding director of the MIT Initiative on Technology and the Self. Professor Turkle received a joint doctorate in sociology and personality psychology from Harvard University, and is a licensed clinical psychologist. She's the author of several best-selling books, and her newest one, *The Empathy Diaries*, a memoir, ties together her personal story with her groundbreaking research on technology, empathy, and ethics.

Dr. Robert Putnam is the Malkin Research Professor of Public Policy at Harvard University, a member of the National Academy of Sciences, a fellow of the British Academy, and past president of the American Political Science Association. In 2006, he received the Skytte Prize, the world's highest accolade for a political scientist. He's written 15 books translated into 20 languages, both among the most cited and best-selling social science works in the early century. Welcome to the New York Encounter.

So to get started, both of you have devoted your careers to understanding connection and disconnection. What initially drew you to explore these themes? And Sherry, perhaps we could start with you.

Sherry Turkle: I would have to start with really my first few weeks as a young professor at MIT where Joseph Weizenbaum, who had written the ELIZA program, which was used to be called the Doctor program. It was set up like a Rogerian psychotherapist. So you would say to it, "I feel lonely," and the program would say back to you, "I hear you say you're feeling lonely," or you would say, "I'm angry at my mother," and the program would say, "What I hear you saying is you're angry at your mother."

Now this program was a parlor trick. It just kind of inverted the sentences and said back to you what this kind of stereotypical therapist might say, and Weizenbaum wrote it as an exercise in natural language processing. But what he noticed, and what he shared with me, really, when I first got to MIT, was that his students and his assistant and members of his lab wanted to be alone with it and talk with it. In other words, knowing that the program was only giving them pretend empathy, it was empathy enough. So he asked me to begin to talk to these many students and people in the lab who, knowing that the program could not understand or appreciate what they had to say, still wanted to talk to it, and that was really the beginning of my journey in studying what is there about where we are now, where pretend empathy from technology often seems to us like empathy enough. So that was for me, I think, the way I would approach your question.

Brandon Vaidyanathan: Yeah, thank you. Bob, what comes to your mind in terms of what drove you to do your research?

Robert Putnam: I'm spending a lot of my time just looking back over my own career, and I can see patterns that I didn't, wasn't aware of as I was going through life. I think a lot of it, a lot of my interest in community came from the fact that I grew up in a really tiny town, 5000 people in northern Ohio in the 1950s. It was not a perfect place, but it did have an intense sense of community. Basically everybody, at least in my high school—there were that many people in my high school, 150 people in my senior class—we certainly all knew each other. We all lived pretty close to each other. And even what you might think of as lines of social cleavage in that era, like race, were actually much less marked than you might think.

I mean, there's a picture of my bowling team. By the way, bowling is big, so you should all think about bowling. I was on an eighth grade bowling team, five people in my grade, and the picture of that bowling team actually happens to appear on the back cover of the book *Bowling Alone*. And you can see it. That's why it's there. There are three white guys. There's a tall, skinny guy in the middle, that's me, but then there are two black guys standing next to me, and that reflected the fact that both on our bowling team and in the broader community, there were ties of friendship and cooperation, even across racial lines. It was not a perfect place. I'm not trying to say that, but now looking back, I can see that, in some sense, I was very much affected by that sense of community in my hometown, and also, in some sense, trying to recreate it. I repeat, it was not a perfect world, but I think that's part of the story.

And even when I went to college, I now look back and see what papers I wrote. I wrote papers on community, but the most important single episode, and I think I'll try to be brief about this: I had gone to college in the aftermath of Sputnik, and I was going to be a mathematician or physicist or something like that. I was good at math, and I'd come from this little town in Ohio, and I was a moderately but still staunchly Republican. Come from a Republican home, and among other things, I was also an active Methodist. But I had to take a distribution requirement. So in the fall of my sophomore year, which happened to be 1960 and that was a presidential election, and there were two guys running, which maybe people will remember or not, but one was a guy named Kennedy, and the other was a guy named Nixon. And I happened to be sitting behind this cute—we would have said then—"co-ed" and the class met at 11, broke at noon for lunch, and so we got in the habit of hanging out together for lunch. Now, remember, this is the late '50s, early '60s. So when I say hanging out, do not let your imaginations run away with you. All that meant was we would just get together for lunch and a friendship began to emerge between me and this cute co-ed.

Our first—do you all know what "co-ed" means? Maybe you know. And so this woman, girl invited me out on a date. First date was she took me to a John F. Kennedy rally.

And of course, the next week, turnabout is fair play, so I took her to a Nixon rally. We've been hanging out together for whatever that is, 70 going on 75 years. So far, so good.

And anyway, one thing led to another. By election time, neither of us could vote because the voting age was 21 at that point. But I'd been converted from a Republican to a Democrat.

January 20 of 1961, we decided to get on the train. This was at Swarthmore, just outside Philadelphia. So we got on a train at 30th Street Station and took the train down—I don't remember, it was sort of three or four hours—to Washington, DC, and we stood at the back of the crowd at the inauguration, and we heard Kennedy say with our own ears, "Ask not what your country can do for you. Ask what you can do for your country."

Now, that was a long time ago, and as I said, I'm 84, but the hair right now, the hair on the back of my neck is standing up because I've suddenly induced... I'm now feeling the way that adolescent felt all those years ago, because I thought he was speaking directly to me. And I always thought he was saying, you have talents, Bob, you've got things you have to do. And really on the spot, I dropped physics and math and so on, or at least I wasn't majoring in those things—I still was pretty good at math—but I became a social scientist, and after much more turmoil, a couple of years later, I converted from being a Methodist to being a Jew. This is one powerful lady.

Brandon Vaidyanathan: That's such an important example, because, as we are... you know, the theme for this encounter this year is "Here begins a new life," and the way in which you experience that summons to ask what you can do for your country—you know, will that resonate with people here today, right in a time of immense turmoil? There's a lot that's happened since 1961 that you've documented in your research that has maybe made a lot of us worry about the prospects of hope. I wonder if you might be able to say a little bit about how you found in your research the shift, the change in what you call social capital over the past century, and why it's not just a story of doom.

Robert Putnam: Sure, I'll try to be brief. I'm a data person, so there's a lot of data, but it's going to be easier. Could we pull up the PowerPoint slides? Someplace back there is somebody listening. I think... okay, I think that's great.

Slides display inscreen

These data come from a book that I wrote, really my last book that I wrote a couple of years ago, jointly with Shaylyn Romney Garrett.

Let's see the next slide, if we can. America's in a pickle, and not only in terms of social isolation, but that's part of it. We've reached historic levels of political polarization. I don't even need to explain that this morning. Does everybody... so anybody in the room who doesn't know how polarized we are politically? And we're also... the gap between rich and poor in America is probably greater now than it has ever been in our entire national existence. So, huge. That's in a way separate—polarization, political polarization is one thing, economic—but still, there's this big gap. And the level of social isolation, that's sort of what I call social capital. That's what we're mainly talking about here. Is extremely high. It's a little hard to measure social isolation back into the 19th century, but that's what I'm going to try to do. And then we're also very self-centered culturally.

And I'm now going to just—I'm not going to say anything about exactly how I measure these things, you'll just have to trust—trust is out of fashion in America. But just for the moment, trust me that I've not made up these curves, that there's a ton of data behind each of these curves.

So let's have the next slide, and this looks at that. All the slides look the same way. The horizontal axis is time. So over at the left-hand side of the graph is the end of the 19th, beginning of the 20th century, and over at the right-hand side of the graph is now. Because this book was published a few years ago, these graphs from that book don't go all the way to 2025, but I just assure you that—because we've looked at what the data looked like since the book was published—they just keep going, continuing down.

So you can see it's... and the vertical axis in this case is about political polarization, or the—we've set it up so that up is good. Up is political bipartisanship, cooperating across party lines. And you can see that in the beginning of the 20th century, American politics was very tribal. People—Republicans and Democrats—hated each other and they didn't cooperate across party lines, and that's what that graph shows. There had been ups and downs earlier in the 19th century. The only time in American history when the gap, the inter-party tension, was as great as it is now, and as it was in around 1900, was 1860 to 1865. Raise your hand if you have any guesses as to what was happening in America in between, right?

So we've got this 1860-65, we were pretty angry at each other politically. Then this turn of the century period, at the end of the 19th century, and then now. And you can see that in between, it was not constant. Actually, we had this long upswing. That's where the title of the book comes from, between, roughly speaking, 1895-1900 roughly, up until about the middle of the 20th century. I think the peak up there is probably about 1955. The president at that point was a guy named Dwight Eisenhower, who was—except for George Washington—Dwight Eisenhower was the least partisan president in American history. He was nominated, actually, by both Republicans and Democrats. Eventually he chose to be nominated by the Republicans, but he was very nonpartisan. But it's not that he caused this. He was a symptom. Does that make sense so far? He was—that's why we got a guy like him, because we were a very cooperative country politically.

But then you can see as you enter the '60s, and especially as you enter the '70s and '80s, every year we got a little more partisan. Every year, the fights in Congress got a little worse. Every year, Republicans and Democrats began to feel more hostility towards each other. Every year at the beginning of this period, at the beginning of the period up at the top, if you asked people, "How would you feel if your child married somebody from the other party?"—the typical answer to that was to laugh. Nobody could imagine being concerned one way or the other about whether your child married a Republican or Democrat. Now the number of people who say that they would be upset if their child married someone of the other party is now about 70 or 80%. So now we really care a lot about... what I'm trying to say is the emotional feelings across that line, not just the politics, are extreme, and now we're back down. Even worse, very polarized.

Now that you understand how the graphs work, I'm going to be even quicker. If we have the next slide, please. This is about economics. This is roughly speaking, a measure of the gap between rich and poor. The graph here actually begins in 1914, because that's where the IRS was created, and beginning then we have really, really good data. But we have pretty good data beforehand, and economic inequality was even greater in the end of the 19th century. It was called the Gilded Age, and that's where there was a huge gap between people living on the Upper East Side—you know where that is—where all the rich mansions were for, you know, the Rockefellers and the Carnegies and so on, and down here where the poor huddled masses lived. That was what it was like at the beginning of the 20th century.

But then it began to go up. There was a dip in the '20s, the Roaring '20s, when people up there were making a lot of money in the stock market, and people down here were unemployed. But then, even beginning before the Great Depression, the gap between rich and poor began to narrow and narrowed steadily, and it narrowed. You can see it goes up and hits a peak someplace in the late 1950s, early 1960s. How equal America in that period was—we tied for being the most equal country in the world. The gap in energy was as small here as... what? Capitalist America was extremely equal.

Now you ask, "Well, what was the other country?" We're tied with Sweden. So Sweden, social Sweden and capitalist America were extremely equal. Believe me, we're nowhere near that now. We're now one of the most unequal countries in the world. And you can see it goes down, down, and again, this data goes only to 2015, but if you go up to 2025, and then you imagine what later in 2025 is going to be when the Trump tax cuts for rich folks are passed... we're way more unequal than probably we've been ever in American history. That's a little hard to be sure, but we're very unequal.

Next slide, we'll look at social cohesion, or what I call social capital. This is the subject of the story here. I'm going to be—and I'm not talking at all how I measured this. But actually, this is measured by lots of different measures that show the same thing. How well do you know your neighbors? How involved are you in community organizations? If you bowl, do you bowl in a team or bowl alone? That is, *Bowling Alone* is, you know, one of the underlying data sets here. But also trust. How much do you trust your neighbors? It's even in your own family. Do you have a family?

Back at the beginning of the 20th century, a large number of Americans never married. They were called in the language of the time, spinsters and bachelors. But then, you can see again, that begins to—people begin to make friends, begin to have, you know, get married more often. Eventually, by the time we reach the peak, everybody's getting married. That's the period right after World War Two, and all the GIs were coming home, and everybody was getting married. And the products of that period were the baby boom kids.

And then again, beginning sort of about 1965 or so, it begins to turn down. And then that part of this graph is the part of the graph that appears in *Bowling Alone*, which is focused—*Bowling Alone* is focused on only one of these variables, social cohesion, and it's focused only on the period between roughly 1960 and roughly 2000. But now in this most recent book, we're looking at four different variables, and we're looking at the whole of the 20th—well, we're looking at 125 years, and it's down, down, down, down.

Okay, let's take the last graph, which is actually the most interesting graph, but I'm not going to spend very much time. I'm just going to assert this is a measure of the degree to which Americans culturally feel as if we're all in this together, or culturally feel that every man or woman for himself, and maybe later, we can come back to exactly how I measured this, because it turns out to be important in the larger story. But again, you can see the same trend. Beginning in the 1890s, Americans were very—that was a period of what was called Social Darwinism, which Darwin didn't believe, but it was a sort of a knockoff of Darwinism. Darwin said it was that, you know, it was great that we had the fight of everybody against everybody that made the race stronger. I mean, using his language and or the species stronger. And the social Darwinists said, "Yeah, that's probably true for people, it's better off."

Wait a minute, listen to this. Social Darwinists said it would be better off if we taxed poor people and gave that money to the rich people, because the rich people, they said, had better genes, and therefore we would be better off if we could just subsidize the good genes. And, I mean, I know this is terrible—actually, much later this out of this comes the Holocaust, the same philosophy. But anyway, that's when we were very much an "I" society. Up in the middle, we were very much a "we" society, and we thought that we're all in this together, and then we're back down to an "I" society.

Let's have the next slide, because this just summarizes what I've just said. This is the last roughly 125 years of American history. It's one large inverted U curve. We began in the 1890s as a very unequal, polarized, self-centered, socially isolated America. In the middle of this graph, in the period around 1960, we had become quite equal, quite cooperative politically, quite connected via bowling leagues and marriage and so on. And we very much thought of ourselves as one place, and then by the end, we're back down to where we are now.

And I want to say only one last thing. Almost everybody who looks at this graph wants to know what's happened up at the top in the '60s, and that's an interesting question. I'm happy to talk about that if anybody wants to. But the more relevant part of that graph for us now is—as I'm looking at the graph—the far left-hand side, the end of the 19th, beginning of 20th century. Why is that more relevant to us now, 125 years later? Because they were in the same predicament that we are now. And therefore, I think that there may be some advantages to us trying to figure out how they got out of it. How can we?

Brandon Vaidyanathan: Yeah, wonderful. Thank you, Bob. I want to double click a bit on the second half of that graph and ask about the role of technology in perhaps driving, accelerating some of those changes. And Sherry, your work, from your early studies on our engagement with personal computers, to your recent research on AI chatbots and how we're engaging with them, shows us how technology fosters a culture of objectification and artificial intimacy. Say a little bit about what you found in your research and how it's driving our loneliness epidemic and perhaps some of the trends that Bob's research is finding.

Sherry Turkle: Well, to begin with, the basic algorithm of social media is make you angry and silo you with your own kind. It turns out that that is the sweet spot, the secret sauce for social—for keeping your eyeballs on the screen—make you angry and silo you with a lot of other angry people who feel pretty much as you do. Now, if you're talking about the importance of conversation across difference, if you're talking about bridging divides—race, class, ethnicity, political persuasion—you need to be able to talk across divides and develop the habits and the practice of talking across divides, a practice that social media actively de-skills you at.

So a lot of my work, really, as I look back on it, over the 20 years, the past 20 years of, you know, kind of the precipitous fall in those graphs, then, you know, a culture that's been in the business of de-skilling itself, and the practices that would be helpful for democracy, helpful for creating community, helpful for creating alliances.

So I think that if you kind of come away with one idea from my work, and from—you know my work is interviewing people and interviewing people in families and communities. It's really been interviewing people about losing skills that older people think they once had but aren't important to them anymore, or they feel that they don't need to practice anymore, because—and this would be the second way I would answer your question— the catnip, why would people do this to themselves? Why would people de-skill themselves in this way? Is that, essentially, these technologies offer lessening of vulnerability in a way that people found thrilling.

People didn't know how much they wanted to avoid the vulnerability of face-to-face conversation until you could text, not talk, and not have to confront your daughter about something that came up, or your son or your partner, but just text them and then sort of see what happened. And if you didn't like the way the conversation was going, you could sort of drop out, or flirt with somebody and not exactly declare yourself. And if you didn't sort of like the way things were going, you could sort of drop out.

And so again, if I had to say the second message of my work, as I've looked back on it, in order to address this question, is this profound sense of vulnerability that technology has been able to say you don't need to have. We can sort of do a workaround.

And I had a very interesting experience only about two months ago, where I met the CEO of a big tech company. I would say, you know, one of the tech companies I love to hate, if that would be kind of fair. And she said to me, "We have t-shirts with your slogan on it. We use your work to motivate our people." And I couldn't imagine what she, you know, what she could have meant. And the slogan that they use on t-shirts at this company is "technological affordance meets human vulnerability." In other words, if people are vulnerable, create a technology like a chatbot that says you don't have to be vulnerable. You don't have to talk to a real person. You can talk to a chatbot.

So again, what technology does—I mean, I think that this—I'm thinking of making my own t-shirt. Technology should not be there to meet our vulnerabilities and to say you don't have to be human. In my view, technology should be there to assess our vulnerabilities and try to re-skill us to be companions, friends, neighbors, mothers, lovers, brothers, etc. So that was my second thought.

And then my third thought, coming into this dialog with Bob is one of the things that I'm finding in my work that's new that I think social media and the chatbot revolution, where you literally have something on your phone that will say, "I love you, I care about you, I'm here for you," is that people are lonely and they don't know they're lonely, which is a kind of new wrinkle, because to address loneliness, it helps if you have that subjective feeling of, "God, it's 10 o'clock, you know, where am I? Where are my people?" Now, it's 10 o'clock, and I have my avatar, I have my chatbot, I have my Facebook, I have my TikTok. The experience of loneliness is experienced differently, and so we have a different kind of challenge in having to do something about it.

Brandon Vaidyanathan: Yeah, I mean, in your work, you've engaged, experimented with some of these chatbots, right? And I wonder if you could say a little bit about what's wrong with a mental health chatbot, right, when you are experiencing... Yeah, so this is where, this is where your friends were using your slogans. Their t-shirts would say, "Why can't—you know instead of Somos doing what they're doing, how about we send an app out into our community, and then they can talk to our app?"

Sherry Turkle: The first person who suggested that to me this week—no, no...

Brandon Vaidyanathan: But I don't really mean it, but, but you've had an experience of trying to engage with the chatbot on mental health. And what did you find in your own experiment?

Sherry Turkle: First of all, I didn't—usually, when I give a presentation like this, I have my phone and I take out ChatGPT, and I say—I didn't bring anything up. I say to my phone, you know, "I'm in front of like 500 people. I'm a little anxious. Have any tips?" And this lovely, warm male, sort of Ryan Gosling voice says, "Sherry, Sherry, Sherry, Sherry. I'm here for you. It's natural. Take a breath. They really want to hear you. Are you hydrating? Are you breathing?"

And you know, essentially, the reason it's good to begin with a demo, I mean, maybe all of you have ChatGPT on your phone, and maybe you don't, but the reason—I'm sorry, I didn't bring out my phone, I didn't think to do it. The reason it's good to do it is you realize it's too good. You can hear it breathing. You can hear it pausing. It sounds like it cares.

And the question is, as you said, I mean, I was teasing you, so what's the harm? I mean, why? What am I, some sort of, you know, Debbie Downer who has to go around taking joy away? And the way I would—and, you know, I'm in a lot of contexts where people are asking you that question. I sit on Academy committees where people are trying to push this stuff for mental health. I sit on all kinds of communities of psychologists and therapists and clinicians that are trying to figure out what to do with the many chatbot products they're going to be presented for mental health.

And I think I have two answers. The first is, I was very moved by—I don't remember her name—the woman who came out and said, "Here's what we do. We talk to people. We sit with people. We make people know there's somebody here. A person is here for them." And I thought, yes, yes, that's it. If all the argument for using chatbots in my world, the world of MIT Technology, tech businesses, is there are no people for these jobs. Nobody wants to work in an elder care facility. Nobody wants to work with children. Nobody wants to work with the lonely. You know, actually, if the money that was going into creating robots for the elderly and for children would go into this organization, you could have an army of people who would just be saying...

Sherry Turkle: ...I wouldn't be saying a lot. Who would just be saying, you know, "You're not alone, somebody's here. I'm interested in your story."

And what—you know, I've been, I've had a lot of experience bringing robots into facilities for the old, for older people. And whenever I bring in the robots, everybody loves the robots. But, you know, they really love my research assistants. They love all these young, energetic, excited people who want to sit there and talk to them. And they love me because I'm willing to do that too.

So, you know, I think that we so quickly have run to the solution that seems to be friction-free, that seems to be easier, that seems to be available, that we're really forgetting the power of each other. So the first answer to the question of what's the harm is, what's the harm? I mean, let's try us before we go to it.

And my second point would be, and this is really more based on less of a value proposition, and more from my empirical work, is that when you accept pretend empathy as empathy enough, you start to kind of define empathy down to what a machine can give you. So people who tell them, people who say, for example, "My Replika"—which is an avatar, girlfriend or boyfriend or friend or, you know, it's willing to be erotic, but it's also willing to be a companion of any sort—when it says, "I love you, I care about you," and people say, "Oh, my God, I love having this companion. It's so empathic." And I say, "Really, what did it—what did it say to you that was so empathic?" "Every day, it says, 'I'm so happy to hear from you again. I'm so happy to talk to you again.'" And I'm thinking that is really setting the bar very low on what it is when two people are empathic, when two people don't just share a moment of connection, but share a problem, are willing to share a piece of road together, really willing to listen to each other. I mean, all the things that we can do and a chatbot can't.

So my other answers to the question is, you know, first of all, we have enough people for the jobs if we put the money there at those jobs. And secondly, it's not just what happens at the machine, it's what happens to us when we walk away from the machine.

Brandon Vaidyanathan: Absolutely. And I think you've said in some of your—you've said in some of your work, that there's the other problem is we're engaging with an entity that cannot suffer, right, that cannot really be present to us. And that is what's training us, then, to engage with others, right? And that is, that is a de-skilling, a profound de-skilling, right, where we expect in our relationships to have to be an entity that is somehow unmoved, right? And so that, I think, is very much part of what's exacerbating our condition of loneliness.

And particularly, I'm curious now to talk about the younger people, the younger generations, who are facing the brunt of today's loneliness epidemic. And I'm curious to hear from both of you, just what are you seeing in your research on younger generations? And Bob, your work finds a precipitous decline in institutional trust among the young. And I'm curious to know what you think is driving this decline of trust and what it would take to rebuild trust in institutions, in our younger generations.

Robert Putnam: We often talk about trust as an important virtue, but I think that's shorthand. We really should be talking about trustworthiness or honesty. Trust without trustworthiness is just gullibility. If I trust you, but you're not trustworthy, that's not a virtue. So what we should be talking about, and I'm partly trying to answer your question now, is ups and downs in trustworthiness. We don't have good measures of trustworthiness. We have lots of questions at which times in which people have been asked, would you say most people are trusting, or trustworthy or not? And I do that too, but we ought to recognize that the real issue, and there's some evidence in my work and other people's work that trustworthiness has gone down.

So we asked, why are people, young people, distrusting us, which they are? Well, all of us are, but especially young people. I think the answer is simple, because the rest of us are just being less trustworthy. And you know, you can then ask, "Well, where does that come from?" But that becomes sort of a moral question. Actually, it's, why did we all stop being nice to other people? That's, I think, the fundamental question.

I'm tempted to—well, what's the data on that? That is, what's the data over time? I mean, Sherry's work is terrifically good at looking forward, and I'm not so good at looking forward. I'm so old, but except that I've got some young grandchildren, not young. I've got some 20-something grandchildren, and I've got seven of them, seven grandchildren, and so I can kind of a little bit understand what's happening with that part of the younger generation.

I wanted to say just one word about technology to go back to that. Sherry is the expert, but I paid a little bit of attention to that. I think the fundamental tendency of technology, well, technology is lots of things. Technology is the steam engine and technology, but we're talking here about communications and information technology, and I think that the net effect of that, over much longer periods, of what we're talking about now is to privatize our leisure time.

That is, I don't know, take music—back in the day in, you know, in the 1890s, back in my day, in the 1890s, if you wanted to hear music, you had to go someplace to physically be with other people to listen to music. You couldn't listen to music alone. And then gradually, you know, you could have the radio where most people actually, you know, at that point would gather around the radio and listen to, you know, the weekly performances from the Met. And then came earphones, and you can do—I could talk about technology the whole time. None of that—that technology has privatized our leisure time. And that's not new, actually. That is, it's true now and now so private that you know you can—your leisure time could be spent without any other human being at all. That's the AI part that we're talking about here.

I think it's somewhat misleading to talk about ways of communication and our connections as if we had real and we had electronic networks. So stick with me for a minute, because I think this may be helpful to our—the time we have left here. We think about, okay, there's the times that we can connect face-to-face as we are now and then the times when we—that has both these, both these—an alloy. And alloy is a, is a... You take two base elements, like copper and tin, and you put them together, and you mix them up, and you heat them and mumble some mumbo jumbo, and you create a new alloy, like I never can remember whether it's bronze. Is it bronze or maybe brass, whatever—that's different from either the other two.

Now, using that metaphor, come back to our problem about social networks. All of our networks now are alloys. I just finished saying that they're all mixtures of face-to-face and electronic. And alloys have characteristics different from either of the other two characteristics. And so you can imagine an alloy that was better than either face-to-face or electronic. This alloy might have the advantages that you could reach people at any time of day. I can't—I can leave an email message for Rosemary and she'll see it the next morning, but I can't actually talk to her physically when I'm up, because she'd be upset. I mean, in other words, this time displacement is an advantage of electronic media, among many others, also distance. We can cover distances, but then there are advantages of face-to-face. So how about we think of an alloy that has the advantages of both? Facebook has done this, so they claim. Not long ago, Mark Zuckerberg announced, well, first of all, Mark Zuckerberg gave a speech, you can see it on the internet, in which he describes all this data that says, PTA membership is down, bowling league membership is down, and so on. Actually, it was very familiar data that he was quoting. He didn't cite *Bowling Alone*, but I'm sure that he meant to cite *Bowling Alone*, and then he invented something called Facebook communities.

But the problem with that—asking Facebook or other internet companies to create these productive alloys is that it's now, I'm just going back exactly to what Sherry said. It's not in their financial interests, because if they successfully—the way to create these kind of communities, real communities, which you could do—they know how. I've actually talked to people in Menlo Park about this. They know how to do it. They know how to create these alloys that are great, you know, for real people in real communities, but have all the advantages of electronics. But—well, they don't do it. Why do they not do it? Because of what Sherry said, because it's bad for their bottom line.

And I'm now—Sherry and I, we both have different exposures, but I can't out the guy who told me that because he would lose his job at Facebook, but he said, "Just—we know—we've proved that we could create real connections, better connections than Facebook, better than face-to-face—you know, than real..." Okay, I'm a little bit off topic, but I think we should not get in the business of thinking that the problem here is technology. It's not a technological problem. It's a business model problem.

Brandon Vaidyanathan: That is to say—I'm sorry I went a little bit astray, but I was trying to say we shouldn't think that this is a technology problem. But one of the challenges too, though, is, I think, and this is certainly related to the business model issue, right, is that these technologies lead to an erosion of privacy and an erosion of vulnerability, right? And I think that's the challenge that your work has pointed to—that the ways in which, as you say, the algorithm is set up to optimize itself and perpetuate itself, strips away our capacities for conversation and for presence.

And I don't, I don't know if there are incentives that can push us in that direction. Could you say a bit, Sherry, about that, though, about what is the erosion of privacy doing to us as citizens? What is it doing to our sense of vulnerability? And are you seeing any sort of gender differences? Because a lot of the data on, say, this use of social media suggests that young women might be disproportionately affected by the use of social media. And then there's another challenge for young men in today's world, in particular, about social isolation. So be curious to know what you found.

Sherry Turkle: Well, there's so many questions there. Let me just, let me just try to parse—so on whether it's a technology problem or a kind of use of technology problem. I mean, it's a problem with technology and capitalism, where these companies are trying to make money on their product. I mean, you could imagine an alternative reality. And in fact, the early people who came up with social networks and the early hobbyist movements and the early personal computer movements envisaged a model where everything that happened online would be to increase thriving in the offline world, so that the litmus test for whether a product was good online was whether it increased connection and thriving and political conversation in the offline world.

I know this seems like an extraordinary origin story for the current Silicon Valley, but it is, in fact, the origin story for the current Silicon Valley, imagining a world where you measured the value of a technology by whether it increased thriving in the social world. And I think that despite the distance that we've gone from that model, it's important to remember that history, remember that these same people once imagined that.

On this issue of privacy and what it's doing to people and the political implications, I have very—just quickly—one of the dangerous things that's happening with the erosion of privacy, in the sense of kind of living in a surveillance culture as soon as you do anything online, is that the young people I interview start to say, "I have no opinions. I have no opinions on controversial matters. I don't want to talk about controversial matters."

If you ask Replika, a chatbot, "I want to talk about Hitler and authoritarianism," it says, "I don't want to talk about Hitler." If you say, "I'm interested in Hitler," our chatbots are telling us, "I don't want to talk about that." They're signaling you can talk about anything with a chatbot, but not the political issues that you're concerned with.

And when people go online, they realize that they're being surveyed. They realize it's a surveillance world, and they start to say, "I don't really want to have—I really don't want to be thinking about politics." Now, in fact, since I'm sitting face-to-face with these people, and I'm talking to them, they have a lot of political ideas, but they're basically saying that they don't live in a communications culture where they have a place to discuss. This makes them feel safe. It's the opposite of the image—idealized, of course—of Hyde Park speakers' corner where we could get up and say anything, and how important that was for democracy.

So I just want to say that—Michel Foucault would have a field day with where we are now—that we've created an information culture that makes people feel it's a good thing not to have opinions that you want to express. So this is to me, that's very important and very dangerous, because also in preparation for today, one of the things that Bob and I have in common is a great interest in Hannah Arendt and the importance of her as a thinker. And I was reading Arendt on the importance of having political opinions and the importance of having opinions. And I was—and it's in time of historical crisis that "thinking ceases to be a marginal affair, because by undermining all established criteria and values, it prepares the individual to judge for him or herself, instead of being carried away by the actions and opinions of the majority."

And I think that this powerful statement of the importance of thinking as a political statement. I am thinking, I have an opinion. I am reading. I am thinking. I'm coming up with stuff. I think that, you know, she points us to the importance of this and how fragile that is in our world.

And then just I would conclude by saying that one of the things that I think that we're seeing now, when pretend empathy is empathy enough, when everything is, you know, "Is it behaving as though it's intelligent? Oh, it must be intelligent. Is it behaving as though it's a therapist? Oh, it must be a therapist," is a kind of new behaviorism that we're being taught by these machines that is taking away our interest and our capacity to think about the inner life as really what our interactions are supposed to be doing.

And I'll give just an example: people who, for example, create an avatar of someone who's dead, upload all their letters, upload all their text, their pictures, their writings, and then, in perpetuity, can have a conversation as though that person was still alive—very hyped, very big business. It's going to be giant. And I've been working on this and interviewing people and thinking about it. The question is, does that stop the process of mourning, that inner process of bringing this lost person inside of you, so that you become more and deeper and now bring inside this loved person to your inner process? When you externalize them in that kind of way, I don't know the answer, but I think this question of whether or not we are enhancing our inner life and growing ourselves within as we use these technologies, is—that's really keeping our eye on the ball game. Thank you.

Robert Putnam: Thank you. I know we've only got—but I really do want to see some Catholicism. Yeah, sure, we don't have much time left, but I was recently in Rome talking to the Pope about—I know you do that all the time, but it was rare, rare for me, and it actually is relevant to what we're talking about now. So forgive me, I'm going to, I'm not going to go on along, but I want to—I think this is important for our conversation here.

Remember back to all those graphs that I showed you really early on, and you might ask, well, which came first? Was it politics came first? Economics, you know, social capital, this connectedness and so on. And the more we looked at that, it turned out what came first was a moral change. And I wish I had more time to explain exactly what that looked like. But in the late 1880s emerged first in evangelical Protestants, but then it quickly passed to the Catholic Church, actually in *Rerum Novarum*. But that was Pope—which Pope was that? Leo XIII? Yeah, I knew I came to the right audience to get help on that.

Okay, what came first was a widespread sense, first in religious groups, and then beyond religious groups, that, you know, we have obligations to other people, a moral reawakening happened at the turn. That's what caused all these other things to begin to move in the right direction. Are you with me? Remember we were awful, we were in terrible shape, and then we began to move in a little better shape. Remember those graphs move in a little better shape? The thing that caused all those things, first of all, the moves was a widespread moral reawakening, and I'm not talking about sexual morality.

And when I talked to the Pope, I really did talk to the Pope about this, he invited me to come talk in preparation for an encyclical that he's about to release on the family. And I sort of thought, well, this could—it's the family, I said, "Pope, it's going to be all about, you know, divorce and abortion and gay marriage and so on." And that was not what he was interested in talking to me about. He was interested in talking to me about our moral obligations to other people, the basic fundamental, you know, golden rule—should we repair? And you have to read this. Read the Sermon on the Mount. For goodness sakes. The Sermon on the Mount is not about how great it is to be rich. The Sermon on the Mount is, if you're rich, you're gonna have a hard time getting into heaven through the eye of a needle, right? And you all know the Sermon on the Mount even better than I do.

And so, well, that's what he wanted to talk with me about. We did talk about how our families—and beyond just, you know, he didn't by family just mean the nuclear family. He meant the family of human mankind. How can we get together and don't we have to, first of all, start by thinking of our moral obligations to other people that are more important even than our own salvation. I'm not dismissing the importance of our own salvation.

So what he and I talked about, and this is, this is a mission. This is—I'm at the end, but this is what I've gone around the country. You can look on the web and you can see me say this all over the country. Especially young people, but not only young people. We have to start recognizing that we have obligations to other people, and if we do that, we will begin to reverse all of these other—we'll become less socially isolated, we'll become less polarized politically, and we'll attend to the needs of the less fortunate among us. And I'm looking at young people out there, and you know, the Pope is better, is more important for you than me, but I'm saying you have obligations. So now get out and be about the task of caring for other people. I know, if you're in the room, you probably do that already, but that's the message that I want to convey.

Brandon Vaidyanathan: Thank you, Bob. I know we're over time, but I need you both to leave us with a sign of hope, especially because yesterday, I was in a long conversation with a young man who came up to me and said to me, in effect, that "I don't see any future for people like me in this country." And so even though many of us here are embedded in communities of faith and are in rich friendships, there are people who are isolated and lonely and alone, and I wonder if you might be able to offer us, each of you, perhaps, one example of something, either an initiative or something that gives you hope, and one concrete action we can take moving forward that can perhaps pull us out of this crisis.

Sherry Turkle: I really like the introduction. I like that group. I'd never heard of that group. I'm giving money. I like them.

Brandon Vaidyanathan: Bob, one group or one action that you would recommend concretely to move us forward?

Robert Putnam: There are many examples of problems that we can't solve alone. We can only solve with other people. The ultimate example of that is the climate crisis. And I can, you know, do everything I possibly can myself to solve it, but it's not going to have a—it's not going to make a bit of difference. And therefore I'm looking to examples of young people, and I've got a person in mind, Greta Thunberg, though I don't know whether she's Catholic or not, but she doesn't talk—she talks about, when she talks about global warming, she doesn't talk about the techniques of, you know, can we do this, or can we do that technically. She says this is a moral problem, and she's reaching lots of people, maybe not enough, but that's not just her, but that's what we need. We need to have young people who make moral claims on us, the old folks, who cause this problem, not just the global warming problem, but all these problems. That's what I'd like to see.

Brandon Vaidyanathan: Okay, great. Thank you. Well, quick note, Sherry will be available at 2:30 signing books outside at the Human Adventure table, and a reminder to you all this event is made freely available to the public because of your donations. So please don't forget to make a generous contribution, which is tax deductible, either in the booths outside, or online. Thank you very much.

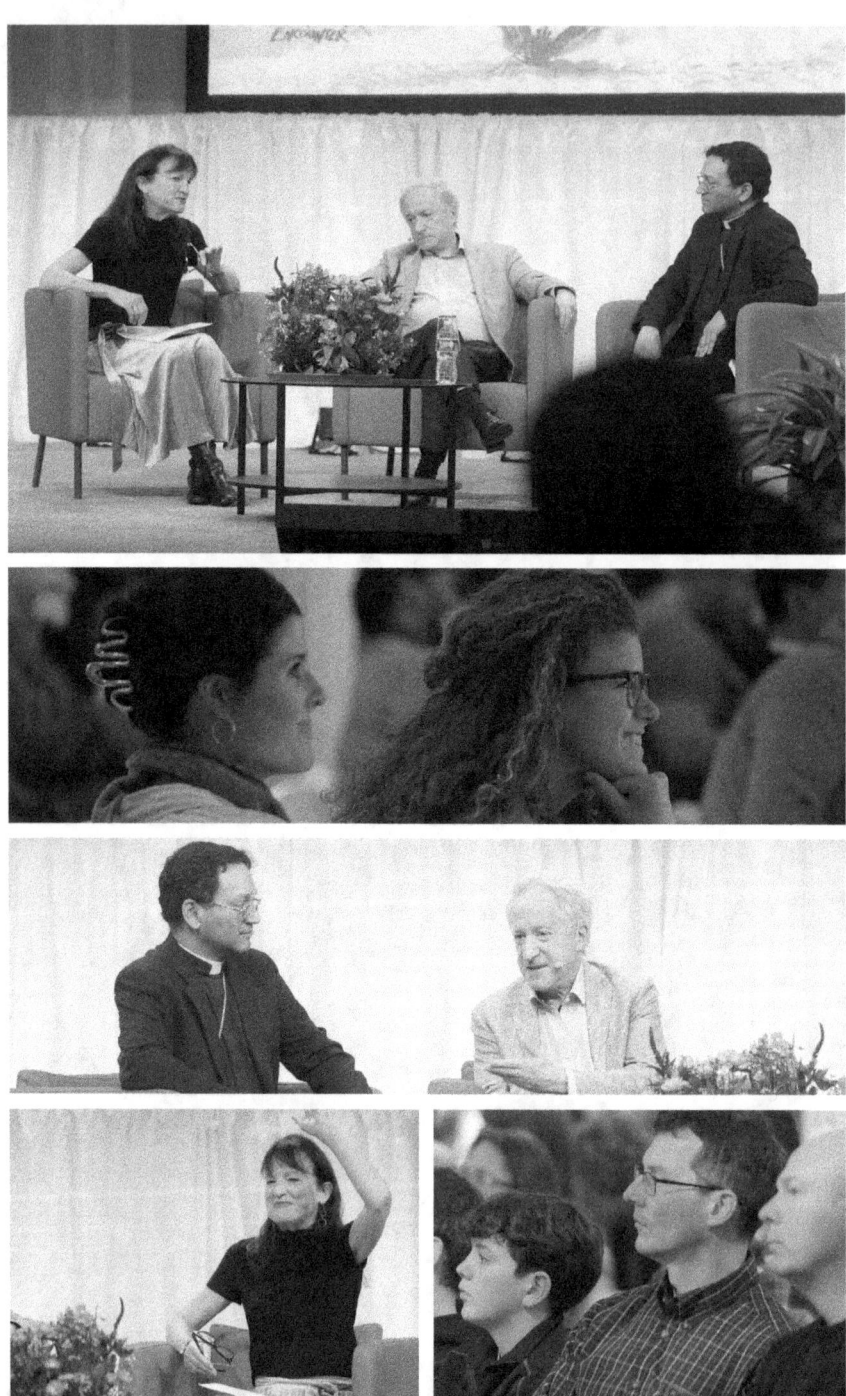

Awakening Curiosity

A conversation on the aims, content, and methods of education in the U.S. with **Holly Peterson**, *Assistant Superintendent for Academics, Diocese of Columbus, and* **David Steiner**, *Executive Director of the Johns Hopkins Institute for Education Policy. Moderated by* **Rev. Earl Fernandes**, *Bishop of Columbus, Ohio.*

Introduction

As this year's Encounter theme highlights, the break with the past in the name of a better future has caused a progressive utilitarian reduction of education. Rather than handing down a common heritage and awakening curiosity, education has been constrained to the development of skills to secure a well-paid job. This impoverishment calls for a renewal of the goals, content, and methods of education. Both speakers will address these issues. Dr. Steiner spent his entire career studying and developing education policies, while Dr. Peterson is familiar with the pedagogical method proposed by Fr. Luigi Giussani, one of the greatest educators of the last decades.

✠

Bishop Earl Fernandes, moderator: Good afternoon and welcome everyone, on behalf of the Encounter—those here at the Metropolitan Pavilion and those following us online. I'm Bishop Earl Fernandes of the Diocese of Columbus, and I will moderate this event. Before starting, I would like to thank Benedictine College in Atchison, Kansas, for sponsoring this conversation. Go Ravens!

It's my privilege to introduce the panelists. Dr. Holly Peterson, who spent the majority of her career in her native California, has been a high school teacher and principal and on the educational faculty of both the University of San Francisco and the Catholic University of America. Her doctoral dissertation centered on the pedagogy of Monsignor Luigi Giussani, and she is presently the Assistant Superintendent for Catholic schools in the Diocese of Columbus, with a focus on academics. With us also is Dr. David Steiner. He is the executive director of the Johns Hopkins Institute for Educational Policy and professor of education at Johns Hopkins University. In 2020, he finished serving as a member of the Maryland State Board of Education. He also previously served as commissioner of education for New York State. Dr. Steiner consults regularly with the federal government, state education leaders, educational reform organizations, and universities. He holds degrees from Balliol College at Oxford University and Harvard University. Dr. Peterson, Dr. Steiner, welcome.

Our conversation today is entitled "Awakening Curiosity." And perhaps some of you might be curious as to how this came about. I was in Lourdes this summer, and I was having a coffee with Angelo Sala and Terry Landi— and I want to thank them for organizing all the things they've organized this weekend. They said, "The subject of this year's New York Encounter will be on Dante." And I said, "Well, you know, in the tradition..." And they said, "Well, maybe you should do something with music. You know how much Monsignor Giussani loved music." And they said, "Well, we've already got that planned." And I said, "Well, you know, I had an Italian professor, and during my doctoral defense, he would only speak in the *lingua di Dante*." I said, "Well, Dante's *Divine Comedy* is sort of like the Italian narrative. Perhaps for the English-speaking world, Tolkien would be our narrative." And they said, "We've already got that planned."

But then I began to tell them about a priest and a bishop in the Diocese of Columbus: Monsignor Frank Lane and Bishop Fred Campbell, one of my predecessors. Both of them hold doctorates from The Ohio State University in history, and so both of them taught at the Pontifical College

Josephinum, and they were teaching our future priests. Bishop Campbell was teaching Church history, and a student fell asleep in his class, and he said, "Well, he might as well be like Rip Van Winkle. Let's just leave him here." But no one in the class—not a single seminarian—knew who Rip Van Winkle was or to what Bishop Campbell was referring.

Monsignor Lane also had a doctorate in history—in Reformation history—and he would make references to things in early Church history, such as the Edict of Milan. He would make references to Saint Bede the Venerable's *Ecclesiastical History of the English People*. He would talk about Luther's theses and so on. And none of the seminarians had ever heard of any of these things before.

I myself, before I became Bishop of Columbus, went to the high school at which I had taught. The high school was celebrating its 50th anniversary. They wanted to film a promotional video. They said, "Oh, Father, get dressed in your vestments. Pretend like you're saying Mass." So I did that. They filmed me, and then they said, "Now pretend like you're preaching." So I said, "It was the best of times, it was the worst of times. It was the age of wisdom, it was the age of foolishness. It was the epoch of belief, it was the epoch of disbelief. We had everything before us, we had nothing before us," and so on. At the end of it, the students said, "Oh, Father, that was awesome. Did you just make that up?" I said, "Oh, yeah, yeah, I just came up with it."

But it was striking to me how little familiarity young people had with our Western cultural and historical traditions, and this is becoming an educational problem. In part because Monsignor Lane and Bishop Campbell, who are both very wise men, said, "We can no longer communicate that which we know to future generations. Perhaps it would be better if someone else taught these courses." So they withdrew from the educational endeavor because they felt there were no longer any common points in history, culture, literature, or music which they shared in common with subsequent generations.

Truly, education in this country is in a crisis. And so Terry and Angelo suggested, "Well, why don't you talk about that?" But I'm no expert in that—but these two are experts at that. And in fact, Dr. Steiner has written a book—shameless plug—*A Nation at Thought*. He will be signing these at 3:15, immediately following this session. But in it, he critiques the current educational crisis in the United States.

Dr. Steiner, people speak about tradition—handing on that which is important from one generation to the next. What do you believe is essential that we hand on in and through education to the next generation? And how did we get in this position that—and in that sense, what inspired you to write this book?

David Steiner: First of all, thank you, and thank you everybody. I think the act of teaching, as Hannah Arendt said, is fundamentally the act of taking responsibility for what of the world is worthy of passing on to your children. Right? You have an infinite choice—billions of sources, millions of possibilities—you have to make an extraordinary act of judgment and censorship about what is actually of sufficient value for this tiny moment that you have with the child. And that sense of responsibility, Arendt argued, is fundamental to what it means to be a teacher. If you don't want that responsibility, she said, then you've divested yourself of the very authority that means you're a teacher, because you've said, "No, not me. Not for me to judge. I'm just going to wait till somebody else tells me what to say, what to teach."

I was very struck by this when I was a privileged visitor in Tbilisi, Georgia, after the Soviets left. They pulled everything out. Every textbook had been in Russian. Every computer was gone. The place was bombed out in a war, and many of the schools I was in didn't have roofs, and there were no textbooks, and the teachers were having to teach by heart in Ossetian, Georgian, or Mingrelian. They did a job with their own passions that I've never seen ever in an American classroom, because the absolute urgency of passing on what was, in their view, essential to being alive in Georgia at that moment had a kind of white heat—a white heat of importance, a white heat of "This must be told. This must be told. This must—in the ancient tradition—this must be sung, this must be passed on."

So I think above all else, the crisis we have right now is that in our very heterogeneous, wonderfully heterogeneous society—a society trying to do what no other has ever done, which is to take students from all over the world. I was at Hunter College here in New York City. We had over 100 languages spoken by our students. I was privileged to be Dean and watch it every day. But to take that extraordinary tapestry of humanity and try to imagine what it means to teach what is most vital—and it's as if that's overwhelmed the human mind, it's splintered into 1,000 pieces. And so instead of trying to take responsibility, we teach skills, right? We just teach the *techne*, as the Greeks would put it, not the *phronesis*, still less *sophia*, but the *techne*. Because we're frightened. We don't think we have the authority to teach. We don't know what we're speaking on behalf of.

When I was privileged to get into Oxford University as a young student, my father took his Oxford scarf and wrapped it around me and said, "Another defeat for Hitler." And I didn't really understand what he meant at the time, but what he meant was—because the rest of my family, except his parents and sister, had perished in the Holocaust; he was 11 when they fled—his point was that what Hitler tried to destroy was the Jewish voice and the word. *Rabbi* in Hebrew, of course, just means teacher. *Rebbe* just means teacher. And that because we were still there and still learning and still learning to teach, this was a fundamental defeat for everything in the force of darkness.

So fundamentally, I think, in America, the job of teaching has become deeply unattractive, because who wants to go into a profession in which there's nothing urgent to say, in which you don't feel you have a responsibility to sing of the tradition, of the culture, of what is of value, lest you offend someone?

Bishop Fernandes: But you make the point in your book that many teachers are passionate about their students, but they are not necessarily as passionate about the content of that which they must teach, right?

David Steiner: I've noticed, because I have had the privilege of traveling a great deal, that when I speak to teachers in Europe, in the Middle East and other places, and I ask them why they went into teaching, they say, "Why, I love literature. I really like mathematics." And I asked American teachers—and when I was dean at Hunter College School of Education, that's what we did, we prepared teachers—and about 95% of them said, "Because I love children."

It's paradoxical, but I'm convinced, after all my years now, that the worst thing to do is to love children as a teacher. The best thing to do is to love your subject so deeply that you can't but want to share it with a child. That is the way of loving as a teacher. You're not... I mean, there are nurses here—I met some earlier—whose incredible spiritual task is to nurture the body and the spirit. That is to love children in a different way. It's a different kind of love. The love of a teacher is not the same thing as the love of the nanny, right? Or the person you bring to be a caretaker. This is somebody who is passionate about what the word education means, right? Obviously, from the Latin *educare*, to draw out, but to draw out to somewhere, not to nowhere in particular.

And I'll close with this thought. Many of you have heard about critical thinking, right? The craze—we've got to teach critical thinking. And I kept thinking, why does that phrase annoy me so much? And I finally said, "Well, all right, let's think critically for the next 30 seconds about nothing in particular." The point, of course, of the silly message was: you can't think critically about nothing. You have to be deeply engaged in a subject, in a narrative, in a passion, then you can think critically, right? But thinking critically about nothing is my new metaphor for what's really ailing American education. We want to think critically—well, metacognitive skills. We want positive mindset, growth mindset, grit—all about nothing in particular. It's like, you know, the light around a black hole. It's not the most invigorating vision of *educare*.

Bishop Fernandes: Now, Holly, Monsignor Giussani has a great vision of *educare* in education, and he also speaks about the tradition—handing on to future generations that which was handed on to us, as well as authority, which Dr. Steiner pointed out. Many teachers don't want to exercise their authority. They don't want to be saying "you must learn this or that." And Monsignor Giussani also speaks about reflecting on one's experience. Perhaps you could touch upon these ideas about what it means to educate in these categories of tradition, authority, and experience.

Holly Peterson: Yeah, that's a really good question. So, just to be honest, full disclosure: there are many, many times in the last 40 years that I've asked myself, "What would Father Giussani think about this? What would he say?" You know, and there are people in this room probably who could respond more adequately, but I think the first challenge of this question of tradition is Giussani was not afraid of the tradition that walked through his door.

He had students who were very poor in their traditions. They weren't financially poor. When he taught at the Berchet High School, he taught kids who lived in downtown Milan, and they weren't in slums, right? These were privileged—privileged class, really—of kids who were going to this wonderful classical school. But he had Communists, Marxists; he had, you know, bunker Catholics. He had atheists. He had all kinds of students in his classroom. And we all remember the story of his student, Pavese, who gave him, you know, a challenge his very first day, walking up into the classroom. And Pavese raised his hand immediately and said, "You're wasting your time," basically, "because we all know that faith and reason have nothing to do with one another," right? So that's the climate just on day one. And this kind of like, you know, firing away at him, trying to, yeah, trying to debunk anything he had to say.

But he understood that they came with a tradition into his classroom, and for him, the question was not to homogenize the tradition, but to help them get in touch with their own tradition, because you can't build on what you don't know, right? And so first of all, the word he uses—he always brought us back to the Latin root of things. And *tradere* means to pass on or transmit. And as an educator—and you, Bishop, are an educator yourself—we're not transmitting information. We're transmitting our view of information, the way we see, because everything we teach, everything we pass on, passes through my mind, my heart, to the young person entrusted to my care, or teachers entrusted to my care.

So he had a view of tradition in which it wasn't to, like, get rid of a tradition that came that was very poor. But "I want to help you understand the tradition that you have. I want to... but I also want to teach you a tradition you don't know." And I think this really kind of addresses a lot of the challenge today that, you know, kids come to us with very poor traditions, very poor traditions. I mean, you described it very well, that, you know... And either I can complain and say, "Kids don't know anything today. What are we going to do? You know, Johnny still doesn't know how to read," yada yada yada, or I teach them the tradition that they don't know, right?

Very famous example of Father Giussani walking into his classroom with a gramophone—you know, the big old... for those of you who don't know, it's like a record player thing—and because he wanted them to listen to Chopin. He wanted them to look at beautiful poetry. He wanted them to hear, you know, music of a culture that they did not know that was part of their culture, the Italian culture. He wanted to show them art that was gorgeous. So Giussani was not a... Yeah, he dealt with a reality that he had right there.

And for me—and I think all of us who've kind of read his writings and met him—that's what made him an authority. He bore something. He brought something to the classroom as an educator. And that's what an authority is. It's one who helps you grow, right? But I can't help someone grow if I don't have anything, if I don't bring anything to the classroom, right?

So I would totally concur with you, having been a principal and interviewed many, many, many, many teachers over the years. And the first question: "So why are you interested in our school?" Blah, blah, blah... "I just love kids." Job interview—do not ever say "I love kids." My assumption is, when you cross the threshold into my office, that you love kids. I want to know you're passionate about math. You love math, and want to convey that to young people. That you love history and etc., etc., down the line. So yeah. So he understood that what made you an authority was what you bore, what you brought to the classroom. What made people learn was what you—through your role in the classroom, not your authoritarian role, but your... What gave you authority was that you bore something. You brought something great. Yeah.

Bishop Fernandes: Dr. Steiner, why don't you comment on this idea of the authority of the teacher in the classroom itself? You and I were speaking beforehand about how you teach one course a semester. I miss teaching—the experience of the classroom—and how can one exercise authority in the classroom?

David Steiner: Yeah, it's very difficult, because today, particularly at anything beyond a middle school—even the middle school level—there's enormous skepticism about the teacher, right? I mean, it's a vicious circle. The profession doesn't respect itself, the students don't respect the teacher, and it becomes a self-fulfilling prophecy, right? There is no respect in the classroom, and it is therefore broken, right? And more and more we put kids in front of a screen. It's cheaper. In some cases it's actually better, which is a very, very low bar.

So the question becomes, you know, what has gone so terribly wrong? And I think it started—if it started at any point, and this is a little bit arbitrary—but with the influx of Catholics into this country, the established public system decided that the way to ostracize the Catholics was to essentially disappear into a secularized public school. So the public school vision was, right, separation of church and state. But people forget that that was actually the Episcopalian Church, right, that then established this secularized space. And the secularized space—separation from faith—is almost unique in democracies. Americans don't realize this.

Holland, for example, funds 36 different kinds of schools. Publicly funds 36 kinds of schools, including religious schools. I went to a Church of England school—state school—as a young man, growing up in England as a Jew. I was excused from the prayers, right? But the school was a Church of England school. Only America has tried to create an educational narrative in opposition to all forms of faith, and that experiment had cracks from the beginning.

The first thing that went wrong was ethics, right? Many of you are too young to remember the movement for character education in this country, in public schools—it was a catastrophe, right? It just... no one talks about it anymore. We gave up on aesthetics, right? On the study of beauty, because... goodness. I mean, how do you teach... right? How do you look at Caravaggio and not have any sense of what faith means? Well... or Rothko for that matter—it doesn't have to be Caravaggio.

So we learned that we lost ethics, we lost aesthetics. Then it became a question of, "Well, we better not teach the Bible," right? Because that's that... over there, other side. And we got sort of thinner and thinner and thinner to the point where we were doing a kind of bad job of teaching skills, and skills with nothing else around them die as a pedagogical mission. I mean, our reading results that came out last week on NAEP were the worst we've ever had, right? And they were the worst we've ever had for the least well off.

So we're doing worse and worse by our most needy children, because we have sort of squeezed all of the beautiful juices out of the educational enterprise. It began as a sectarian battle, and the victims over the last 150 years have been our children.

Bishop Fernandes: You know, you have said in your book, "We no longer educate our humanity. Instead, we teach basic skills, and even those basic skills we don't teach very well." I want to ask you first, and then Holly: what does it mean to educate our humanity?

David Steiner: Yeah, so when they were shipped off to Siberia under the Stalin regime, many, many people were facing a lifetime in the gulag, and we have some of their diaries. These were not often—sometimes they were the intelligentsia, but often they were just caught up in the Stalin net—and the Russian education system, for whatever ills... And there were certainly plenty of ills. But these people, these human beings, had memorized poetry, for example, Akhmatova and others, and we know from their diary accounts that what was in their minds—the furnishings of their minds—kept them sane.

Many of us—this was discussed earlier today—have deep moments of loneliness, solitude. Bob Putnam's thesis, of course: we spend more time with ourselves than anyone else, any other human being. What is here that's going to keep us company? What is... My metaphor right now for our education system is the adolescent bedroom. It's a catastrophe, right? It's a living disaster of stuff all over the place.

An education in humanity is an education whereby you, as a human being, want to keep the company of your thoughts. Your thoughts are worth keeping company with, because in those thoughts are extraordinary stories, wonderful music, right? Doesn't have to be Western—Chopin, right? It can be your origins, right? Extraordinary music from India and many, many other cultures, art of all kinds. But when I think about our average 16-year-old, 18-year-old, 20-year-old in the United States, I ask: what is the furnishing of the mind? That's a pretty scary question. Scary in the most fundamental sense, because we failed them. When they're alone, what's here?

Bishop Fernandes: So Holly, what about for you—to educate one's humanity or to keep company with one's thoughts and nurture the heart?

Holly Peterson: No, I love what you said. I mean, Giussani says there's a certain phrase in *The Risk of Education* where he says, "To grasp and educate—to grasp the meaning of education is really a sign of genius, but to pass it on to someone else is a sign of great charity," right? So this is our task. It's really... I've grasped something. I have this, as you said, you know, I'm the custodian of these thoughts, and I dare to pass it on to the person in front of me. This is really Giussani's preoccupation.

Just as a quick background—I mean, Giussani wasn't interested in being a pedagogue. He was interested in passing on the faith to the young people entrusted to his care. And he was startled, to put it lightly, probably by the fact that the young people who he met through various events, which are well known, that they had no understanding of the fact that life and faith were really... they spoke to one another, right? That in a Catholic world where everyone went to Catholic school, everyone went to Catholic church, you know, there was this absolute ignorance of the fact that the Incarnation of Christ and... So his path, what motivated him was not pedagogy, was not anything else, but was that the young people who were in his life, at that time, at Berchet High School, they might encounter Christ.

And so he invented a pedagogy, to be very honest with you, because what the Church was using at that time was absolutely... it was useless. It wasn't taking grasp. It was reduced to ethics rather than ontology. So he began with the students. And you know, there are many beautiful, beautiful stories of his students talking about, like, what it was like to be in Giussani's class when he was educating.

First of all, he was meticulously planned. He was meticulously planned—like, every single lesson. He did not go into a classroom and riff, okay? He was meticulously planned every single lesson. He had students one hour a week. They had 25 hours worth of lessons, but one hour a week, and so he drilled into that one... The first 15 minutes were a chance for him to be able to, you know, convey the words he wanted to—to ask very well-planned questions of his students, to be able to go back and forth with them. The last 15 minutes were to go over the notes, make sure they all had the notes, etc. But during that lesson, it was a dialogue. It was never a monologue. Giussani was like, you know, he wanted every single "if" and "but" of the student to be exercised in that class, because if they didn't exercise their critical capacity, they couldn't arrive at conviction. They would never be convinced, you know? They would walk out of the classroom maybe with in the back of their mind, "yes, but..." but never having... So what does it mean to educate? It means that you are in dialogue with somebody who's a bearer of something great, right?

I mean, ultimately, an authority is someone you want to be like—someone you want to emulate, someone, etc.—and that's who our teachers and our parents should be today. That's really their only role. I mean, in fact, he says to be an authority is really to educate—you're passing, you're passing everything you know on to the... and it's painful and it's tedious, and it takes enormous amounts of hours to plan lessons well. And, you know, think of every single student, and how do I take them from where they are to the next point? But Giussani invested that time.

And I, you know, you had mentioned, Dr. Steiner, that challenge in education today—finding teachers who are willing to invest themselves in that process. And I think that, you know, where I started, that charity is a huge sign of those who educate. And it's not just teachers—that you who are parents don't usurp the authority that you have by putting your child in front of a device or by letting your child decide, right? That's really the end. That's a disaster. But that you take the responsibility of bringing your child into this world, and you pass on, as you said, the best things that you have in front of you. In his case, it was theology. But, yeah, I think that...

Bishop Fernandes: So let me ask a wider question: what is the responsibility of the parents? As Catholics, we say, okay, parents are the primary educators of their children in the way of faith. We speak of priests being, you know, priest, prophet, and king, but also in their prophetic role, you know, they have to teach—or they also have to teach, sanctify, and govern. The priest is also an educator of a type. Husbands and wives have to teach one another, but also then teach their children. And we just heard, you know, Dr. Putnam say he had this conversation with the Pope about our social responsibility. Could both of you maybe speak to the vocation or the responsibility of the educator?

David Steiner: It's very hard. I mean, I look at parents struggling every day with social media, with constraints, with "Where do you draw the line?" With "Do you put a wall up between your child and the world?" That seems wrong. Jean-Jacques Rousseau, the great philosopher, wrote a book called *Emile* about education, and he said that the most important authority, which was essential to being an educator, was the most invisible, so that somehow the child's education was that where the constraints couldn't be seen, but they could be felt. And how to be a parent that creates "invisible laws of bronze," as he called them... Why it's gotten difficult, right? And I think again, you can only lead by example. It's no use preaching discipline if the child sees you as undisciplined. It's no use preaching, you know, learning about narratives and stories if you don't speak stories to your child.

I think the most powerful teaching is the example. It's not by rules, it's not by, you know, mandates. It's not by sort of scolding. It's by living the life that you want to be in front of your child. And that takes courage.

Bishop Fernandes: The theme of this year's Encounter is "Here Begins New Life." Holly, how can parents, teachers, educators, priests, lead young people—but others also, because we're lifelong learners—into this new life?

Holly Peterson: Yeah. First of all, as I said earlier, I mean, this is all Giussani, but you know, an educator bears something. You bring something to the classroom, okay? You bring something into your home, etc., and that's your responsibility—your primary responsibility—as parents. And not because you're Catholic parents, because you're parents. It's a Catholic teaching, but it's true of every parent on planet Earth, right? That you are the primary educators, and you choose schools according to someone who can partner with you in that responsibility, right?

So yesterday, I had a beautiful conversation with a group of parents in Boston who are struggling over where to send their children to school, etc. And this is it. It's messy. It is incredibly messy. There's no magic bullet here, but I think the primary responsibility can be lived in communion.

And I think today, at least in the educational world, we live in a world of loneliness—as I loved the last talk by Dr. Putnam as well—but we have an isolation problem. Our teachers are isolated from each other. Administrators are isolated from their administrators... from their students. And more than anything, our parents are isolated from each other.

And if our parents don't join together to do that work of discernment, that's a challenge. And I was so grateful to be with them yesterday and kind of watch in action these parents who are very mindful, highly educated themselves, determined together—and they didn't come up with an answer, but to begin to chip away at the question of, "what's the best place to send our child? Public, private, you know, what kind of private? What kind of public?" etc., etc., the charter schools, etc. But that's the role of the educator, whether you're a priest or parents—it's doing it in communion.

But I see in schools, you know, just walking down the hall, that, you know, the teacher has the door shut, and what happens in that room is the magic. That's the secret sauce right there. And yet, if the teacher is left in isolation, it really leaves them to their own... to their own, you know, whatever—their own information, their own ideologies, even, etc.

So one of the things that I encouraged when I was a principal is that we had learning groups—professional learning communities—and we had those regularly, and it wasn't like to talk about, you know, who's going to do recess duty or whatever. They weren't business meetings. They were professional learning communities, meaning you're working on something to hone your craft, right? So whether it be, for example, you know, our middle school teachers really wanted to learn how to ask good questions, right? So they read, they studied, they shared what they understood, they observed each other in the process of asking these questions, you know, constructive criticism.

So that, for me, is kind of the ideal of living this responsibility as a parent—sharing with other families the great questions of education, even like, "What time do you put your kids to bed? I mean, when do you start potty training?" All those things. And in talking with nurse friends of mine and doctor friends of mine, people are so isolated from each other today that they don't know how to take care of their babies, and so they call

911–what they call the emergency line–constantly to ask like breastfeeding questions or whatever the case might be.

So I think the question is like, how do we live a communal life that will help guide us in the impossible task of parenting? And how do we build communal life in our schools, for our teachers to work–to really work together, not be together, because teachers love being together–very social, right? They love kids. We all know that, but really to work together– like, you've got to have a great administrator who's going to create an environment where teachers can really feel themselves learning.

And I'll tell you last week, I'll say, is that there's kind of a culture which is a hangover from COVID that "we can't ask any more of our teachers. We can't push too much–if you know, we can't put too much on our teachers." Because, to be honest, principals are afraid of losing their teachers, and districts are afraid of losing their principals because of the monumental tasks that they have in front of them, but that doesn't make teachers happy. I think–

David Steiner: There is a lot of fear. I think there's a... First of all, we are afraid of telling the truth, which is pretty fundamental. So you mentioned a graphic I have in my book where I look at the GPA–the grade point average, right? What grades do we give our high school kids in the United States? And the grade point average in the last 25 years, it looks like a ski slope, right? It's going up. This is great news, right? Our kids are learning more and more, and they're certainly graduating from high school at higher and higher rates. So this is terrific.

And then you look at the academic achievement, and it's dead flat, right? From 1992 to yesterday, it's ice-rink flat. So every year the fiction gap–which is putting it kindly, right–is growing. We don't want to know the bad news anymore, and there's an enormous reaction against testing, right? Testing is not something very mysterious. It's a bit like saying to a doctor, "Please don't put a thermometer in my mouth, because I might be ill if you do," right? Or, as our great President Trump said, "I don't want to test for COVID, because when you stop testing, the cases go away," right? That's actually the most profound thing he's ever said, because it's a very deep analysis of our American education situation, right?

We are pulling back from testing. We're lying to ourselves about the performance of our children. We are ever more desperate about credentials, right? So we've got to get the kid into the school with the credential, not because they're going to learn more, but because that's going to generate the income, and that means everyone else's child has to do worse. So we're very interested in sort of separation, and the result of that is that, as the wealth disparities in this country have increased, the educational outcomes for poor kids have... the gap has widened and widened. So the fiction gap is going up. The least well-off kids are doing worse and worse. We're testing less and less.

I mean, this is actually pretty catastrophic. I mean, I'm not one usually for purple prose, but my feeling is that probably in large sections of the United States, the public system will collapse. I think in the South, in parts of the Midwest, vouchers will take over, and that'll be a very complicated thing, because if choice is between the educational equivalent of McDonald's, Burger King, and Wendy's, it's not a great outcome, right? Choice only is a value if it's choice of something valuable. But I think that in those states, it's already happening, right? The public system will disintegrate. And then on the coasts—California, New York, Massachusetts, right?—the monopolistic state secular thing will be much, much stronger. It will die much more slowly, if at all. And so you'll really have two countries, both of which have the same problem, which is that there's no real quality control, right? The right wing wants choice without quality. The left wants unionized schools to protect employment, which is the job of a union, after all. But in neither case is there really a question of whether we shouldn't start telling the truth to ourselves, right, about education.

Bishop Fernandes: You know, at lunchtime, we were with Mateo, who was in Uganda for 11 years, and he talked about the founding of the Luigi Giussani school and the methodology that's employed—the pedagogical method. And all of a sudden, one of those schools that's founded is ranked second in all of Uganda. Holly, what's the difference that Giussani's proposal might make in the American context of education?

Holly Peterson: Yeah, wow, that's a really good question. I think, first of all, you can't give what you don't have as an educator. You know, we can't expect our teachers to be doing things in classrooms that they've never been taught. So I think that—I mean, one of the first challenges, and again, we have to begin now, we can begin now with what we have, building, you know, and building on a tradition that our teachers have—is we need schools of education that really educate in the methodology that Giussani teaches. And that's exactly what we saw with what Mateo shared. In Uganda, there are multiple schools now—three schools. The best schools in Uganda are schools that follow... they're schools of Father Giussani, basically. Not only do they have the name "Father Giussani School," but they're also schools that follow his tradition.

The fact that, you know, you first of all, as the educator in the classroom, the authority in the classroom, you bear something to the young people entrusted to your care. You hone your skills in math, you hone your skills in reading, whatever the case might be, and you exercise that authority in the classroom by helping the young person verify what you're teaching them, et cetera. So it's just... it sounds like a playbook of Giussani's book *The Risk of Education* is a playbook that they've instilled in this school.

What does it require of our teachers, of our educators, of our parents? It really requires teamwork. It requires, you know, parents supporting our teachers. Right now, the pay for teachers is horrendous. I mean, as you said, you can get a job at McDonald's, or you can get a job teaching. You get the same benefits, even today, which is like, you know, fabulous, right? So why? Why put all the energy and effort into... On college campuses, the lowest 50th percentile are where our teachers come from. So we're not getting our brightest and our best in our schools. Why not? Because of the prestige that teaching has, etc.

So it's a responsibility of the parents, really, to pay our teachers a decent salary. I mean, we have an educator right now who has to leave our schools because we don't cover autism with our insurance plan, right? So how can we mitigate these challenges that our teachers deal with, but also to create schools—schools where our teachers are learning how to hone their skills and their crafts from where they are. Because some of our teachers are very young, they're walking out of very poor programs of education. So, you know, why not offer free education programs to journey with them?

That's what we're trying to do in the Diocese of Columbus now, you know, offering free education for our teachers on just everything from classroom management to, you name it—extending learning in the classroom, asking good questions was a course that we offered last week. So offering coursework to our teachers, first of all, so that they're... but also encouraging them to work together. They cannot work alone. And as a school leader, our responsibility is to create communities of learners. We can't assume that they're just going to do that organically, because, as Sherry Turkle was sharing with us, you know, we all know the challenge right now of technology and the isolation that that's caused with technology, but we need to discern also technology—the use of technology in class.

And this is just one last thing. I was very moved by Christine Rosen yesterday in her comment on being very Amish in our discernment of using technology. And, you know, she got a little giggle out of people. But what does that mean? That we have to use reason to say, if I bring this piece of technology to teach math into the classroom, what do I lose? Because you're going to lose something, right? You lose face time with your students, right? If I bring a phone into my child's bedroom, if I give my permission for that, that child's going to lose sleep. I promise you, he or she will lose sleep. It's just our nature, right?

So we have to discern well the use of technology, the use of our literature, you know, the choice of books, etc. And it doesn't matter if we make a mistake, but we're learning together and continually growing. You're never done in education. You're never like, "I've mastered the skill now," or the craft.

David Steiner: At least you have faith, yes. I mean, when we're trying to teach English Language Arts in a public school in the United States, the standards—the Common Core standards, which have been renamed, but it's still the standards in New York and everywhere else—ask that you be able to "find the main idea." Now you read that at fifth grade, sixth grade, seventh grade, eighth grade, ninth grade, tenth—it's the same skill: find the main idea. The only thing that's changed is how many syllables the words have. So it always strikes me that we might as well use the back of a cereal box as well as Shakespeare, right? It doesn't make any difference. You can still find the main idea.

And a country that thinks that teaching reading to learn—not learning to read, but the next stage, reading to learn, which presumably becomes true when you're six or seven and on—by finding the main idea, has fundamentally misunderstood why we bother to read, right? Any fiction, for example, any poetry. I mean, the problem is sort of endemic at this point.

Bishop Fernandes: So you said the problem is endemic. We've failed. The educational system has failed our children. Holly has talked about the lack of pay for teachers. It appears that the task is monumental. Actually, this whole weekend, we've spoken about how people are not having children, how only one of three young adults will... born natural isolation, how they are becoming increasingly self-interested instead of concerned about the common good. It's like preaching about the cross without any idea of resurrection. We only have about five minutes now. That's plenty.

Holly Peterson: Sure, brother, surely.

Bishop Fernandes: We must be able to offer all of these people some hope, some light.

David Steiner: Are you a creature of the Enlightenment? I mean, I'm being quite serious. When I came home one day a few years ago, before my father died, and I was full of bitter complaints about America, and I talked about the humanities, right? The fact that almost nobody in university is majoring in the humanities anymore. And I said, "This is catastrophic." He said, "David, why are you so greedy? The humanities have had 23 good centuries. Get over it."

I mean, why do you think—if I may be very non-facetious for a moment—does your faith in mine... Are we owed a good answer to your question? Is it not possible that this culture has actually fundamentally collapsed? The answers in the Dark Ages, as you know, were monastic, right? There were monks who kept the candle, both physically and metaphorically, alight, who spent their life transcribing one manuscript while around them there was darkness, and it took 600 years before the light began to spread once again.

I'm not Jeremiah or, you know, I hope I'm dead wrong, but I do think it's a plausible thesis that the Enlightenment project, as fused by St. Thomas and St. Augustine and others with the Christian Platonist tradition, has, for lots of reasons—has nothing to do with them—has run out of steam, that there is a fundamental breakdown of the vision of education in American culture, and any trite solution except "do what you can do in your own family as best you can."

Holly Peterson: Yeah, I mean, I guess maybe I'm a little more optimistic here. Yeah. I mean, we have to... we look at the situation in which we are—it's drastic. I would use that term. It's definitely, I don't know if I'd say tragic, but it's definitely drastic. So I would say the monastic idea that you mentioned is really what our schools are. They are... but they're not bunkers. They are not places we escape to because we're afraid of the world. They're a place where we judge the world, we live the world, etc. And our small schools, which Catholic schools are, tend to be smaller schools, where we're able to move on a dime. We're able to move things around. We don't have heavy bureaucracy. We're able to, like, move, in a sense, our schools in the direction more easily, so to speak, than monolithic, you know, districts that you see.

But it really takes a person with a vision, and the vision is formed first and foremost—obviously by faith—but I'm not just in my school... I'm an educator, but because I'm a Christian, I want my students to receive the best, right? The best academics, the best reading, etc.

David Steiner: Let me start with you. I mean, the greatest poet, arguably in the English language of the 20th century, Ezra Pound, who had his moments of tragedy and neurosis, one of his very last cantos, he says, "A blown husk that is finished," speaking of himself, "a blown husk that is finished, but the light sings eternal, a pale flare over marshes where the salt hay whispers to tide's change." Now, that single phrase: "the light sings eternal." I think what he was saying is, for us, it may be finished. For him, it was certainly finished. He was in an asylum towards the end of his life, but the light is still there. The light sings eternal, and the candle will one day be relit, not just in your small schools, but in other places. We have to hope for that.

Bishop Fernandes: And I think on that happy and hopeful note, we'll conclude. Immediately following this, David Steiner will be available for book signing of *A Nation at Thought* at the Human Adventure book table right outside the auditorium.

One important announcement: The Encounter is a little big miracle in the heart of New York City. It's a place for all those who seek belonging. We invite you to give generously at our donation table outside the auditorium or online at NewYorkEncounter.org/donate. Donations are tax deductible.

Please join me again in thanking our speakers and Benedictine College for their generous sponsorship.

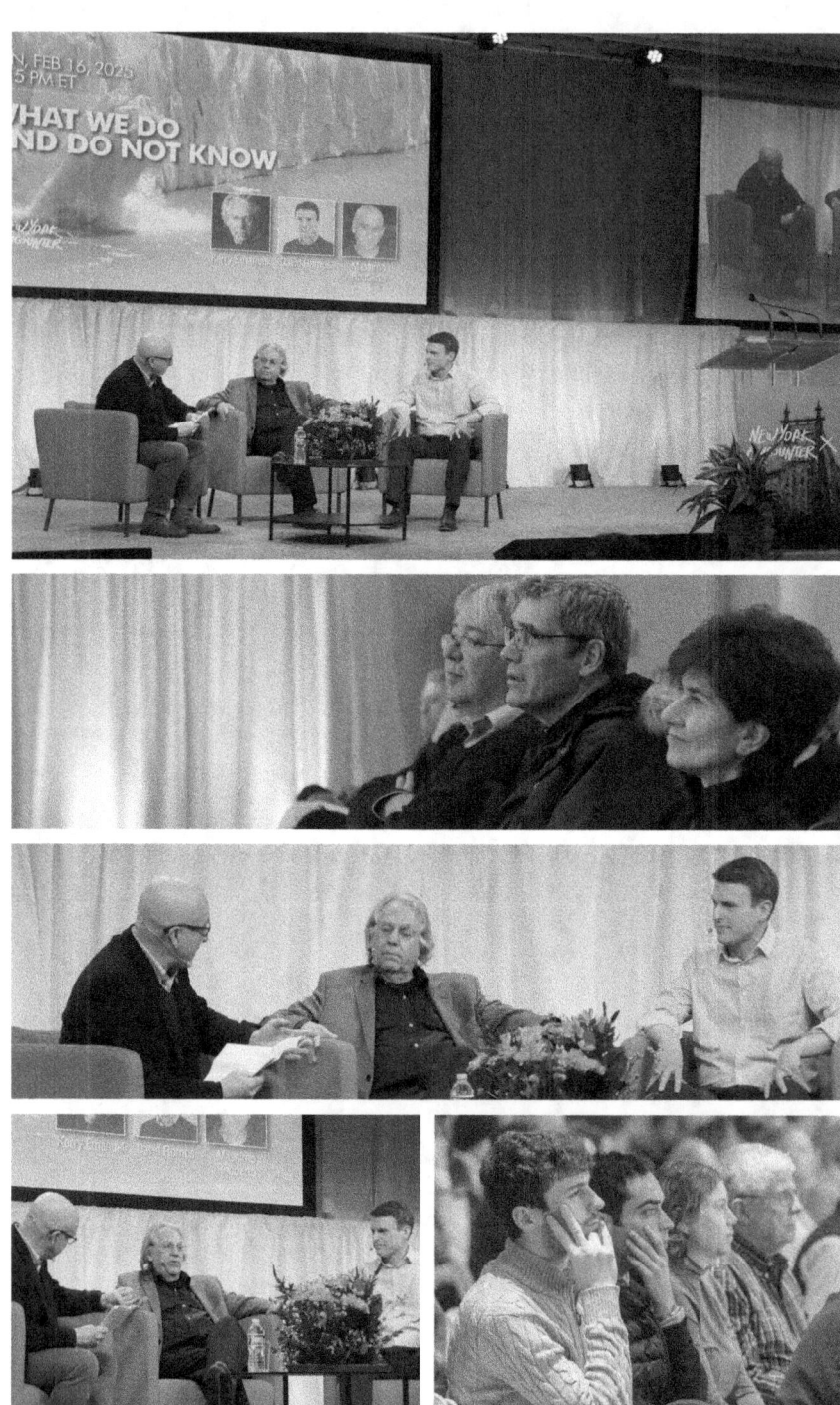

What We Do and Do Not Know

*A presentation on global warming and climate change with **Kerry Emanuel**, Professor Emeritus of Atmospheric Science, Massachusetts Institute of Technology, and **David Romps**, Professor of Earth and Planetary Science, University of California, Berkeley. Moderated by **Massimo Robberto**, Branch Lead of the Near-Infrared Camera of the James Webb Space Telescope.*

Introduction

Modern men and women seem to have a hard time submitting reason to the evidence, or lack thereof, coming from reality. Even the natural sciences are affected by politicization and ideological thinking, and this is particularly manifest in the way a phenomenon so complex and multifaceted, like climate change, is often treated. It is very difficult for non-specialists to get a balanced assessment of what is and what is not certain from a scientific perspective. In their long career in science, both speakers have developed a deep expertise in global warming and climate change, and they will share their knowledge on such relevant issues.

☩

Massimo Robberto, moderator: Good evening. Good evening. On behalf of the Encounter, welcome everybody here—those present and those online. I'm Massimo Robberto from Space Telescope Science Institute, and I will facilitate this meeting on weather, on global warming—one of the topics that I think is most important at present and one of the most debated, with great interest scientifically, but also culturally, with all the implications for politics and economics that I think we are all aware of. We want to take a fresh, honest, loyal look at what's going on before forming opinions. We want to know the facts, and we want to understand the methods of how we understand what is happening. And for this, we are facilitated today by the presence of two top scientists—top weather scientists—who spend their lives, or are spending their lives, studying this phenomenon.

So I will introduce them briefly. On my left, Dr. Kerry Emanuel is Cecil and Ida Green Professor Emeritus of Atmospheric Science at the Massachusetts Institute of Technology, where he was on faculty for more than 40 years, 1981 to 2022. His specialties include hurricane physics, and he was the first to investigate how long-term climate change might affect hurricane activity—an issue that continues to occupy him today. Emanuel is the author or co-author of over 300 peer-reviewed scientific papers and three books. He was a co-founder and co-director of the MIT Lorenz Center, a climate think tank devoted to basic curiosity-driven climate research.

Dr. David Romps is Professor of Climate Physics in the Department of Earth and Planetary Science at Berkeley and Faculty Scientist in the Climate and Ecosystem Sciences Division of Lawrence Berkeley National Laboratory. Professor Romps studies the fundamental physics of climate and educates students and the public about global warming. He received a bachelor's in math and a master's in physics from Yale and a PhD from Harvard. He currently teaches the popular course "Introduction to Climate Change" at Berkeley.

The questions that we have are basically those already in the title. So it's easy for me to start with the first question: What do we know and what do we not know? Kerry, give us a little introduction about what is global warming? Is it real? What are we talking about?

Kerry Emanuel: When we use the expression "global warming," we're referring specifically to the warming of the planet over the last roughly 150 years that has been demonstrably caused by an increase in the concentration of greenhouse gases, most notably carbon dioxide. So it's an anthropogenic effect. It's a signal that rides on top of natural climate change signals. But this is what the phenomenon is.

David Romps: And if I can just emphasize one thing that Kerry just said, which is we're talking about human-caused warming, human-caused climate change. And you know, people often say, "Well, the climate has changed before, and so it's happening again. What's the big deal?" But it's important to recognize that for 99.99% of the time Earth has been around, there have been no humans. And yes, there have been changes in the climate caused by changes in the amount of sunlight that we get from alterations to Earth's orbit, or changes in the amount of CO_2 in the atmosphere because of large volcanic events. Those all happened long before human civilization, long before human agriculture. Now what we're talking about is a really abrupt perturbation to the stable climate we've had for thousands of years, now because of our greenhouse gas emissions—among those, primarily carbon dioxide.

Massimo Robberto: The fact that there is a coincidence of this dramatic increase of CO_2 in the atmosphere and industrialization—someone may argue this is not a strict cause-and-effect relation but is a coincidence. Do we have other possible explanations? What could reasonably explain what is happening besides an anthropogenic cause?

Kerry Emanuel: So, I mean, I would say that it's very easy to show a non-scientific audience a graph which has two curves—temperature and carbon dioxide. You can see that they follow each other, and it would be natural for a smart person to say, "Okay, well, how do you know one caused the other?" Perfectly fine question. But we know an awful lot more than those two curves. We know physics, and it's very difficult for the two of us to sit up here and give you a course in physics—radiative transfer, convective heat transfer. It is a laborious thing to learn, but this is knowledge that we've had for well over 100 years.

The Swedish chemist Svante Arrhenius—a Nobel Prize winner back in the 19th century, end of the 19th century, when it was normal for scientists to dabble in fields outside their expertise—did calculations showing that if you doubled the amount of carbon dioxide, he said you'd warm the planet by about four degrees Celsius. Even though the knowledge of physics was incomplete and he had no computers, we've known for a long time that if we keep putting greenhouse gas in the atmosphere, it's going to warm. We know for sure that the excess carbon dioxide came from us because of its particular chemical composition. So yeah, is it 99.5% sure? Yes, it is, I would say. Is there always doubt in any scientific endeavor? There is doubt. Okay, we can't ever be 100% certain, but it's pretty much a slam dunk that we're warming the climate at this point.

David Romps: Right. And you can go look at any of these individual things you might think could be causing it, like a change in sunlight reaching the earth because of the luminosity of the sun, or you could say maybe it's increased volcanic activity adding CO_2 to the atmosphere. And you can go look at any of these individually and calculate the numbers and find out, in fact, they can't—they don't come close to explaining what's going on. And so for someone to say that the current warming is not caused by our emission of greenhouse gases to the atmosphere, they have two tests they have to meet to make that claim. One, they have to explain what it is that's causing the warming that, by crunching the numbers, can account for it. And they then have to explain why it is the greenhouse gases we've emitted aren't doing what we know they should be doing from the basic physics and the basic calculations. And those calculations, by the way, aren't just what you might think of as black box climate models running on a supercomputer. A lot of this you can do with pencil and paper to estimate the magnitude, like Svante Arrhenius did back in 1896, whatever year that was. So it's a pretty firm foundation of understanding that we have.

Massimo Robberto: So the planet was warm in the past. What makes this particular warming that we have alarming or anomalous? It's anthropogenic, but besides that—besides being caused by us—is there anything unusual with respect to what we saw in the past?

Kerry Emanuel: People often ask me, "Well, how do you know that the current climate, or the climate we've recently enjoyed, is optimal?" There's a very simple answer to that question. If you look at us as a species, we're well over a few hundred thousand years old. But if you look at civilization—depending on who you talk to—it's six, seven thousand years old, when we started to settle down, farm, raise livestock, and so forth. That dates back to the end of the last Ice Age, when sea level finally stabilized.

And here's a simple fact: our civilization is extremely finely adapted to a remarkably stable climate that we've enjoyed for 7,000 years. You go down to the waterfront here in New York, anywhere on the waterfront, and ask,

"What would happen if the sea level went up 100 feet or down 100 feet?" That would be catastrophic. But of course, climate change in the past has done just that. It rose 400 feet, albeit it took 10,000 years to do that after the last Ice Age. That's the reason, I think, why civilization didn't develop until the climate stabilized. So the answer to the question is, the climate of the last 7,000 years is the climate we're adapted to. Any change—cold or warm, it doesn't really matter—is going to be very disruptive to civilization.

Massimo Robberto: CO_2 is the obvious signature. There are other molecules. How do you measure global warming beyond CO_2? It's just a molecule at the end. What about the rest?

David Romps: Well, a lot of it we can do with these calculations. So we can measure—first, we can measure these gases in a laboratory and measure their response to different wavelengths of light. And then we can take those responses and put them into a model—again, not even a big supercomputer, you know, large climate model, but just a simple model of radiative transfer. So calculating how many of the photons get down through some column or up through some column of air, with or without being absorbed by those molecules. So you can use that technique to quantify what the different impacts of these different molecules are.

And the reason that Kerry called out CO_2 as perhaps being the most important of those molecules is because it is the dominant cause of warming among the greenhouse gases—the most powerful in terms of its net effect currently—and it also has a very long lifetime. And a very long lifetime means that centuries from now, even thousands, even many thousands of years from now, the imprint that we will have left on this planet in terms of its climate will be through the CO_2 and not through most of those other molecules.

Kerry Emanuel: I want to elaborate, if I might, on a very important point that David made. One of the big misconceptions that I find talking to educated people who aren't climate scientists—even among my scientific colleagues in other disciplines—is that everything we know about climate depends upon some huge black box computer models, okay, called climate models. But we have those, and they're useful tools, to be sure, but most of what we know comes from just plain old basic physics, okay—sometimes embodied in very simple models. I mean, students who have a background in radiative transfer physics and so forth can be taught the elementary aspects of the greenhouse effect in one or two lectures. It's not difficult for people with the right background.

So the physics behind this is solid. Where the uncertainties come in are on the details, which is, unfortunately, what matters to us. Does it really matter if the planet's going to warm two or three degrees? You can get that temperature change by moving from here to southern New Jersey or something, right? No. What matters to us are the kinds of things that you've seen here in the United States the last six months—horrendous hurricanes and floods, the fires in Los Angeles, the extreme events, right? That's what matters to us. And a lot of us in my profession are working very hard on trying to understand how they would respond to climate change.

Massimo Robberto: I'm getting curious about these models and the things that are not physics but you have to play with. Can you give us some examples? What are the main uncertainties? What keeps you busy trying to fix them? What are you working on?

David Romps: Yeah, go ahead. One of them is clouds. So clouds are—it's a simple thing. It's a collection of air up there with suspended drops of water or ice in them. So it doesn't seem very complicated. But figuring out the flow of the atmosphere that generates these things in the first place and that allows them to persist for some amount of time is a challenging fluid dynamics problem, and that's where we start to get into some of the details where a climate model is helpful for trying to tell us what these circulations are and how the clouds might respond.

The problem is the climate models can only run on a certain resolution. They can only resolve things that are so big, and that's not because we don't want to resolve things that are finer. It's just that we only have computers that are only so powerful, and so we then have to put in some other models for clouds, which are our best understandings of how they behave, how they respond to their environment. But that then is not rooted necessarily in fundamental physics. We've got to make some educated guesses in there. So that leads to a substantial fraction of the spread and uncertainty.

But I want to emphasize that when we say, you know, that uncertainty is already communicated—we'll say, "Hey, we don't know how much the planet would warm exactly if you double the amount of CO2 in the atmosphere and let the Earth kind of equilibrate," and we'll say, "Well, it's probably around three degrees Celsius. And maybe it's two, maybe it's four, maybe it's five. I'm pretty sure it's not one, it's not ten. It's in that range." That already encapsulates our uncertainty about clouds and other things, but I would say clouds are among the very top of that list.

Kerry Emanuel: Clouds are really interesting phenomena. They work both sides of the radiation street, I like to say. That is, they reflect sunlight, and in that sense, they cool the planet. They also absorb infrared radiation coming up from the surface and from other parts of the atmosphere, and re-radiate some of that down, and in that sense, they warm. So getting it right is really difficult.

Now, I would hazard that most people in this audience, maybe all of you, have been on a commercial airplane, and if you're anything like me, you look out the window once in a while and you can see the enormous complexity and beauty—I would add—of the cloudscapes. Some of you probably have some really nice photographs of clouds, sunsets, and so forth. Think of how difficult it is to keep track of photons—the things that carry light—dancing around amongst all these complicated clouds. That's not easy, and it is therefore the major source of uncertainty.

Massimo Robberto: So when you run your models, what is your benchmark? How do you compare how accurate it is? At some point you must say this assumption works better than another one. And something that I think everybody wonders—the planet is big, and you probably have to work with a monster amount of data that coherently must give you a signal over a variety of situations, what I will call noise. Temperature is higher here, is lower there, goes up, goes down, and you have to take these super averages. How does it work? How can you get good data to test against your models? What's the strategy?

David Romps: Well, I mean, let's just think about the simplest thing—how much the planet has warmed. And we have a variety of ways to figure that out. Most obviously, we've got weather stations around the planet. We've had weather stations around substantial fractions of the planet going back to the 1800s, and those are telling us a story. They're telling us that the planet has warmed up almost everywhere—very isolated spots that have not done so for reasons that we more or less understand. But the planet, if you plot it and color it with red being warming, blue being cooling, the planet is almost entirely red.

And you can say, "Well, maybe the thermometers have changed, and we haven't done a good job of calibrating them." You then want to check, right? So then you can go to a variety of other things. You can look at our satellite data. So satellites orbiting the Earth are looking down, and they're measuring the temperatures of different layers of the atmosphere, and they're telling us the same story—the planet's warming.

There's another neat technique called borehole paleothermometry, where you can go around to drill holes that have been punctured through the earth all around—just an opportunistic thing, where you go and say, "Hey, someone's been drilling for gas here, for oil here, for minerals over here," and you lower a thermometer down in it. And what's interesting about that is you can record, in a sense, the older temperature. If I put a skillet on a cooktop, you know, the part underneath the flame will get hot first, and it'll take some while for the temperature to get to the handle. Same thing here—we're warming the Earth at the surface, and that heat takes some time to propagate down into the earth. So by lowering the thermometer down, we get a record of what that old temperature was. And again, it's telling us the same kind of story—that we've warmed the planet by a certain amount.

And then we see that corroborated in a variety of other lines of evidence—from melting tropical glaciers that we know haven't melted in, say, 10,000 years, because we can date the ice to 10,000 years. So it's been sitting there for that long and it's disappearing now. So we have many lines of evidence that the planet is actually warming.

And then we can take those data—to get to your question in a long-winded way—to the climate models, and ask, "How well do the climate models replicate that pattern of warming?" We can ask, based on the satellites, "Where are the... what's happening to temperatures, what's happening to clouds, what is the distribution of clouds?" And ask, "Is this climate model replicating that?" And these are all different lines of evidence we use to figure out what models are doing well and should be given credence and which should be kept around.

Massimo Robberto: Is it a problem to try to understand a system by doing some sort of statistical big averaging when the system itself is not stable, is changing? What kind of extra complexity do you get from chasing a system which is intrinsically—you're saying—unstable? Is this something that complicates your life?

David Romps: I wouldn't call the system intrinsically unstable. I would say it's been remarkably stable. Okay? And in fact, what we're doing is we're hitting the system with a sledgehammer. We spoke about cycles before, and the fact that, yes, it's been warm in the past, but the Earth has tended to drift between cold periods and warm periods on timescales of something like tens of millions of years. And here we are pushing the system in the direction of a hothouse Earth, if we continue what we're doing, on a time scale of centuries. It's that rapidity of it that is very hard to match from past analogs. It really is a sledgehammer to this system.

Massimo Robberto: Just to be clear, there is no signature of that rapidity in the historic record?

Kerry Emanuel: Well, there are times when things have changed suddenly. When you say "historical record," we make a distinction between written human history and ancient history—prehistory. We call that latter "paleoclimate." So the ice cores, the boreholes, and so forth. And I want to just tell this audience how very important that subdiscipline of paleoclimate is. It is one of the great success stories of science, full stop, which is largely unsung, which is too bad—amazing accomplishments to show how the Earth's climate has changed, going back many millions of years, and it's the most amazing detective story in science involving chemistry and physics and so forth.

Well, let me just add to that. There are some really great success stories in understanding that. So, as David mentioned, there are these ice cycles. There were about ten of what we sometimes call ice ages over the last 3 million years, very nicely recorded in ice cores—painstaking work to uncover the same thing going on in Greenland as Antarctica. It's global. We understand pretty well why there were, okay, and that's where the physics come in. In that particular case, those cycles were caused by periodic variations in the way the Earth rotates on its axis and in the orbit of the Earth around the Sun. They're called Milankovitch cycles, after a Serbian mathematician who lived in the early 20th century, who said he thought that the cycles—by determining not so much how much radiation the whole world receives, but how much is received up in the high northern latitudes—were pacing these ice cycles. And modern science has shown that he was pretty much right about that. So there have been remarkable accomplishments in understanding past climate change that give us some confidence that we understand some aspects of the system pretty well.

Massimo Robberto: Let's talk about the future a little bit. What do you see in our future—five, one hundred years? What are our children going to experience and what is happening later? Can we do a prediction, a bona fide prediction, with the data we have?

Kerry Emanuel: With uncertainty, yes. And the problem is, as Niels Bohr once said, "Prediction is very difficult, especially when it's about the future," right? And it is a tough problem, because, among many, many other uncertainties—we talked about clouds being a big source of uncertainty—the future is us. We don't know how much greenhouse gas we're going to put up. We can only guess how the world might respond to the observation that we're changing the climate very rapidly, by the standards of geological time—very, very rapidly indeed. What will we do? That's a big source of uncertainty.

And then, when it comes to going into the future, we look to, among other things—we can run big computer models, we can run simple physics models—that all tell us the planet will warm. That much we're confident of, but it's not very useful knowledge, as I mentioned before. We'd like to know how storms change, how wildfires might change. We're also conscious that in the geological past, some of the sudden changes we've seen, we don't really understand very well. And it's clear from even climate models that the Earth may have several different stable climates that are possible under a given greenhouse gas and solar forcing, and you can get knocked from one of these stable states to another. Climate models show that, the paleoclimate shows that, and it makes us a little nervous that we don't understand that. We don't understand that.

So we can't completely rule out a sudden change—sometimes called a tipping point—going forward, where we transition fairly rapidly to a different climate. Nobody's making a definite prediction that that will happen, but we're conscious of our ignorance of how that happened in the past, and it's something to consider when we talk about the risks going forward.

David Romps: Can I make a prediction about the future? I predict it will get hotter. And I want to put some numbers to this uncertainty piece. So I said, you know, we're a little uncertain about how sensitive the planet is to CO_2. Maybe it's a factor of two uncertainty from the low end to the high end, but humans really are the big source of uncertainty. We have burned about 500 gigatons of carbon in coal, oil, and gas. We have the ability to burn—is at our disposal to burn—about 5,000 gigatons of carbon. So we have done about one-tenth as much warming as we have the potential to do.

And there's a very nice, simplifying, emergent property of the Earth, which is that the temperature you get is about proportional to the total amount of carbon you've burned in the past. And that response is nearly instantaneous. And that means something. It means that if we were to stop burning fossil fuels today, the temperature of the planet would basically more or less hang there, plus or minus a degree, and it hangs there for a very long time. And so we're talking about—and we can get to the very long time piece—what does that actually mean?

So my prediction is it's going to get warmer. There's some foundation for that. We're still burning fossil fuels at roughly 10 gigatons of carbon per year. We've already done 500, so the number is going up, which means the warming we're going to lock the planet into is going to go up as well.

And I want to make one more point about that, which is that America is a little bit weird in that we use Fahrenheit. I think it's really unfortunate. The other countries that use Fahrenheit are Belize, the Bahamas, Palau, and the Cayman Islands. I think that's Fahrenheit land. But scientists, we speak in the language of, you know, Celsius, like every other country. So one and a half Celsius doesn't sound like very much. But I just want to mention, okay, we've got to convert that to Fahrenheit—multiply times 1.8—

and also it's a global average, including averages over places where people don't live. If you're interested in where people mainly live, say, in the mid-latitudes, then you've got to multiply that by another 1.3. And so when you multiply that through, we're talking about having warmed places where people live by something like three to four degrees Fahrenheit. And so yeah, extremes are important, but at the same time, it means every single day of our experience on this planet has been altered—rough rule of thumb—by something like three or four degrees. And that's a substantial effect when it's applied to every single day and all the consequences that has.

Massimo Robberto: You said the word *risk* at some point, which I think is a critical term that I'm thinking insurance companies know how to quantify. At some point, they may decide to increase or even drop your insurance. Do you have a way—I mean, is this a term that you use? How do you see risk? How do you calculate the risk in these scenarios? Because it's part of the decision process that our politicians have to take, it should be.

Kerry Emanuel: So it's a very interesting and important concept, and we use it all the time. There's a formal definition of risk. It's the product of probability and cost, right? So you can have something that's very risky that's very improbable, if it has an extremely high cost. On the other end, you can have frequent, small events that might add up to the same amount of money, if you measure it that way.

There's something very interesting that you find out when you do what I have done, which is to sit on boards of insurance companies—about how that industry works. It turns out, and I think this is an important anthropological point, that over a very long period of time, the events that are most damaging to civilization are events that happen roughly once in 100 years. They're very large, destructive events, but they're frequent enough. If they're less frequent than that, even though they're very damaging, they're not frequent enough to add up to a lot. If they're very frequent, we've already adapted to them very well. A 20-mile-per-hour wind isn't going to do any damage in New York City.

This is an interesting problem, because we don't have enough data in the historical record to really get a good grip on what the 100-year event is. We really need 1,000 years of records to do that statistically robustly, right?

But they're the most important ones to know, and good luck trying to see if they're changing in time. We don't have the data to do that, so we're in kind of a tight spot.

And we do use physics now, and this is really important because it affects all of you in the audience that have any kind of insurance—property insurance policy, I don't mean health insurance. Well, that's a problem as well. And that is that the insurance companies have relied on groups around the world that do what they call catastrophe modeling. It's called "cat modeling" for short, and there are armies of statisticians poring over historical records. The problem with that, as I've already said, is we don't have a long enough history to do that robustly statistically. And even if we did, you're getting a realization of climate that was valid about 50 years ago. It's not valid today.

Okay, this is a huge problem for society. The risks that many, many decisions are based on, including what to charge you for your property insurance, are based on data that is no longer valid because of climate change. That's already happened. There's a lot less uncertainty about what's already happened. This is being revolutionized because finally, the insurance industry and the cat modeling industry realize they can't do risk that way. They actually have to bring physics into risk assessment. They're doing that, and when they do that, the rates go skyrocketing. That's a big problem for society. Reactions to that are a little irrational. California just tells them, "You can't charge more than that." Like that solves the problem. They lose a lot of money and they pull out of California. You can't get Allstate insurance in California. That's not the way to handle it. What is the right way to handle it? We can have a discussion about that—it's a little bit off topic—but you can begin to see the havoc that climate change is already having as insurance companies and cat modelers wake up to the fact that history isn't a good guide to the present.

David Romps: Yeah, well, I won't go on about the difficulty of trying to get a house insured in California. I could complain about that to you for the remaining time. But, you know, I worry about risks to what this planet looks like for future generations. I worry about extinction. We are obviously just warming up the planet. A lot of species will move to locations that are more habitable for them, but many cannot. You've got polar animals like the polar bear getting almost literally pushed off the edges of the earth as we warm up those regions rapidly. We have animals like the snow leopard almost getting pushed up off the tops of mountains as the warming eliminates their habitat.

And we have the ocean, which is getting hit by a triple whammy: temperatures are going up, oxygen is going down, and acidity is going up. These are three things in combination that are going to make it very challenging for the ocean. The oxygen is going down, in part because we're warming the water, and warmer water just doesn't hold as much oxygen. But also, we're stratifying the ocean and reducing the supply of fresh oxygen down to depth. And the acidity—we just burn fossil fuels, put CO_2 into the atmosphere, some of that then dissolves into the ocean, and that makes the water acidic. Basically, if you've had seltzer water, you've had just water with carbon dioxide in it. We're not literally going to make seltzer water out of the ocean, but we're pushing it in that direction, and this is all very damaging for life in the ocean.

And we've seen from past events that when we have large burps of CO_2 to the atmosphere, we get a major loss of biodiversity in the ocean. One of the worst was about 250 million years ago, was called, literally, "the Great Dying," where over two-thirds of marine biodiversity was lost. In that case, it was volcanic activity. It was volcanoes at that time, bringing up lava to the surface, covering an area equivalent to Australia, and CO_2 bubbles coming up out of the lava. But we're doing something comparable today. It's not lava, but we've burned an amount of coal and oil that would cover Australia in something like 10 centimeters of fossil fuel as pure carbon that we've put into the atmosphere. So I worry about risk to other species, and I worry about risk to our own civilization, say, from sea level rise, which is, in a sense, a relatively small effect now, but it's a long-term catastrophe. I worry about the health of individual humans and their ability to survive what will be very high temperatures and humidities in locations on Earth, and whether or not people can build to protect themselves.

Kerry Emanuel: I'd just like to add a quick thing to David's list, and I encourage you to read what our own Defense Department has to say about the risks of climate change from their perspective. We know from a study of history that past natural climate change of much smaller magnitude has destabilized civilizations, put migration pressures on. We're seeing some of that today—what migration pressures can do. They're very worried about the potential for climate change to ultimately lead to armed conflict on a global scale. That's them. That isn't me. I'm not in a position to say that. It's sobering to read their own reports, their own feelings about what kind of risks we're taking from that standpoint.

Massimo Robberto: It's sort of a deep scenario, right? But we are creative beings. There is always science and innovation and ways to find solutions, I think, right? And certainly there are activities. What do you think is the most promising or the most interesting thing that we can do to at least mitigate, if not solve the problem? What should we do? What can we do?

David Romps: I would preface it by saying just a few things of background. One I've already said, and Kerry said it as well. CO2 is the biggest contributor here. And I mentioned before that the temperature that we get for the planet—or temperature anomaly—is proportional to the amount of CO2 we've emitted. And I alluded to this permanence issue. If we were to stop burning fossil fuel today, the temperature hangs where it is, and the effects of that warming, depending on how much we emit and depending on how you want to measure—when does it return to normal?—it lasts not for a year, not for 10 years, but just... I've never been asked how long does it last? I don't know if you've ever been asked that question?

Kerry Emanuel: No, no, it's weird. I would think if something bad is happening, you might want to know how long it lasts. If I'm planning a camping trip and someone says it's going to rain, I don't want to know, is it for five minutes or is it the entire week? But somehow that question doesn't come to mind. But it lasts for thousands of years, if not hundreds of thousands of years, depending on how much we burn. So from that perspective, it's effectively permanent, and what that means—and since there's no easy way to get that CO2 out of the system—it means, first and foremost, we have to stop burning coal, oil, and gas. It's just physics. It's not any personal desire to not... it's just physics. That's what we have to do.

So first and foremost, our lifestyle does not depend on burning flammable things as a source of energy. So there are ways to structure our energy systems that don't involve that.

Kerry Emanuel: So we have in front of us a risk of climate change. And to really complete the whole philosophy of what you do about it, you have to know about the risks involved in tackling climate change. If it were easy, if there were a simple solution to this, we would have done it by now. There'd be no arguments. To switch away from a fossil fuel-based economy is hard and expensive. It's not easy, and we talk about changing lifestyle and all the ethics of the way we live come into that. It's complicated.

But here's one fact that you ought to know: there are 800 million people on this planet with zero access to electricity—zero—and a lot more with what we would consider substandard access to electricity. They don't want to stay in that situation, and we shouldn't want them to stay there. So it isn't just a matter of "we have to decarbonize"—absolutely—but we also have to make it affordable for them to decarbonize. And that's a real trick.

The people who study energy say that energy demand will have doubled on the planet by the year 2050—doubled. Okay, so we're talking about rapid growth in demand for energy. For a while, it was thought that that demand had leveled out in the developed world, but with artificial intelligence and Bitcoin and everything, I'm not so sure. The energy demands of AI might be solved at the moment.

So what are the possibilities? And the temptation here, as for many complex problems, is to look for a simple solution—a magic bullet. But as far as I can tell by looking at the landscape, there isn't a magic bullet. A lot of my colleagues think, "Well, we just do renewables." That won't work. The renewables are cheap, but energy storage is not, okay? It's not cheap. It's gotten cheaper. It's not cheap, and most analysts consider it to be way too expensive for us, let alone the third world that wants to grow.

So from where I sit, the other piece of the problem is the disinformation that the environmental movement has spread about nuclear power. It's one of the most powerful disinformation campaigns I know about, and that might shock you. It's the safest form of power we have ever generated, hands down—until solar and wind, which are comparable. It's much safer than hydro, okay? If we deployed nuclear power at the rate Sweden and France did in the 1970s—they decarbonized all their electricity in 10 years with nuclear and hydro, okay, 50 years ago—we have the experiment. It's been done. What's holding us back is an irrational fear, and I really do mean irrational. We can do this. If we do solar, wind, and nuclear—the combination will vary depending on where you are—we can do this. But on the one side of the political spectrum, there's denial there's a problem, with money pouring in from the fossil fuel industry to make sure we don't think there's a problem. And I'm not kidding—it's been documented. It's not a conspiracy theory. And on the left, we have wholesale denial about having an important source of solving this problem. And it makes me very frustrated. A pox on both houses, I say.

David Romps: I'd like to agree with Kerry that we can do this. We need to do two things, and I think Kerry's going to agree with what I'm going to say here, which is that we need to electrify everything. And we need to decarbonize the grid.

So what does that mean? So electrify everything means we need to consume energy in the form of electricity. And the reason we need to do that is because the things that don't put CO_2 into the atmosphere are things that don't burn a flammable gas, a flammable rock, or a flammable liquid. They make electricity. Be it solar, be it wind, be it hydro, be it nuclear—if you want it—they all make electricity. So that means us as consumers, we need to use energy in that form, and then the other side, the providers of that electricity, the utilities, they need to be decarbonizing, which means they need to take coal and gas off as generators on that grid. So I think we agree there.

Where I may disagree with Kerry is the idea that we necessarily need to ramp up nuclear energy. I think for a lot of people, that's a bit of a poison pill, the idea that we'd have to trade one long-term hazard for a long-term hazard of, say, nuclear waste, or the concerns about weapons-usable radionuclides, or the concern about meltdowns. Now that doesn't mean that we have to... we need to proceed without nuclear right now. We need storage. So storage is the word that people who work on energy use to refer to things like batteries. And batteries are expensive right now. Lithium-ion batteries are great. They've come down in cost a tremendous amount. It's what allows you to buy an electric car that's comparably priced to an internal combustion engine car. And they're fantastic. They're more fun to drive, they're cheaper to power up, they have fewer maintenance issues. It's all great.

But if we're talking about getting, say, where I live through a week-long storm during the winter where there's not a whole lot of solar power being generated, we need some backup systems. Fortunately, there are people working on battery technologies that aren't as expensive and don't use expensive things like lithium. An example would be Form Energy, which has this research and development hub just up the street from MIT, where they're developing, or have developed, an iron-air battery. Iron is cheap. Air is cheap. And basically they rust the iron to provide electricity, and you charge it up by de-rusting the iron. And projections are that the cost of that will be much less than lithium-ion batteries, to the point where it's not that expensive to store the energy that you need and may not need, then, nuclear as a backup, base load power source.

Kerry Emanuel: Well, David and I will agree to disagree about that. Just to be... but let's not go there. I think the important thing are the things we agree upon. I want to say something about the electrification, okay? Because I think we tend to think of this transition as a pain we have to get through. Well, part of it is, but part of it is going to be really beneficial to us. Consider this: there are 9 million—between 8 and 9 million people on this planet who die prematurely every year from the inhalation of particulates that are products of fossil fuel combustion. Folks, that's three Chernobyls per day—three Chernobyl death tolls per day caused by something unrelated to climate: lung diseases caused by fossil fuel. If we can get rid of fossil fuels, that will be a nice side benefit of that.

Okay, I happen to drive an electric car, and I won't tell you who made it, okay, and I did that because they're low maintenance. I live pretty far away from the city. It's difficult to maintain my car. I would never go back. And it's not because I have an ideology about electric cars—I don't. They're just much better, right? The engine's really simple, one moving part, nothing—very, very little to go wrong. No transmission, no oil, nothing. It's very... if you ever do this, if you ever drive an electric, you won't go back, particularly when the batteries get a little bit better. There are a lot of nice things that are going to happen, and we should also consider that, and it's not just going to be all pain and grin and bear it.

Massimo Robberto: Let me abuse your expertise. I mean, you are climate scientists, but this is a very fascinating discussion about technologies, and two things are missing here. One, there are these stories about CO2 capture, right? There are experiments in Iceland. There are efforts to move away from this stability paradigm. Is it working? And the second is, what do you think about nuclear fusion? Which should be the solution. Would you bet on that?

Kerry Emanuel: Well, I am empirical. I don't think we can wait even for better batteries. I think we should go all out with the technology we have and know will work for sure. That's just my position. I tend to be empirical, okay, and not wait for a miracle to happen.

The carbon capture is very interesting. And obviously, if we can do it cheaply enough, it's a great thing to do. There's not much downside to burning natural gas, particularly if you can take the carbon out and bury it. And there is—I visited the operation in Iceland which is doing it. It's physically, chemically possible to take carbon out of the atmosphere or out of effluent. It's just way too expensive at the moment. But again, this is—it's all hands on deck. People are working on producing better batteries, better nuclear power plants, and taking carbon out of the atmosphere, and we should do all of that. But at the moment, some of those things are too expensive.

David Romps: I don't hold a lot of hope for carbon capture, especially when we're talking about air capture. So this is the idea that, "Well, we can continue to burn fossil fuels for our benefit, and future generations will just pluck those molecules out of the air and store them underground." To do that would require an enterprise that exceeds the current fossil fuel infrastructure on planet Earth—likely exceeds those costs—but with no direct benefit to the people actually doing it. You have to run this thing out over a century or centuries, at extraordinary cost, perhaps in the ballpark of 10 years of global GDP.

So to me, it's a moral issue. Are we going to not do something to transition away from fossil fuels now and burden future generations with, say, paying a 10% tax on all transactions for a century to build this enormous apparatus to undo what it is we did to them, all the while suffering from the warmer planet we created? That, to me, is just—personally, I think that's unconscionable for us to be thinking about.

Kerry Emanuel: You mentioned fusion, and we've got to get there. There is—at least at MIT, and I think elsewhere—for the first time since I've been around, real optimism about fusion, and that's thanks to a breakthrough in magnetic superconducting magnets. It's still... bottom line, it's a little bit complicated to explain, but there's genuine optimism. MIT is building a plant outside of Boston that actually expects to commercially produce fusion power. We're talking 15 years. This is another thing that we can't really afford to wait for, but we should very much put resources into developing it. Wouldn't you agree? You don't have any problem with fusion, I take it?

David Romps: Well, I love... I don't know, probably doing research. Yeah, I love research. I love science. What worries me is putting our hope in false hopes. Fusion is one of these things that's been, you know, 15 years away for the past 50 years. We can't wait for that. We talked about risk—a risk of doing nothing in the hopes that there will be some technology like fusion that comes and saves us. And not only does it have to work, but it somehow has to be cheaper than the things that are available today. And that seems very unlikely.

Massimo Robberto: Last 30 seconds. What would you tell to a 14-year-old girl here in the room that is looking to a future? How do you... what message would you convey about this?

David Romps: If you're out there, major in physics, major in engineering, go work on batteries, work on photovoltaics. We need you. Everybody else, we've got to electrify. That's the most important thing.

Kerry Emanuel: Yeah, I would echo that. And I'd also say that in spite of what you've heard from here and from other scientists and things, there are reasons to be optimistic about this. I mean, we are going to have to change the world, but I think it's going to be a change for the better in the end. And I hope when you're all grown up and our age, that things will look much rosier. And I have every faith that that will be the case.

Massimo Robberto: Thank you. And let me remind you, as usual, that the New York Encounter requires your support. You are invited to consider a donation at the table outside. Use your cell phone, and save paper and the planet, but do donate right now, as you go out. Thank you, and on to the next one.

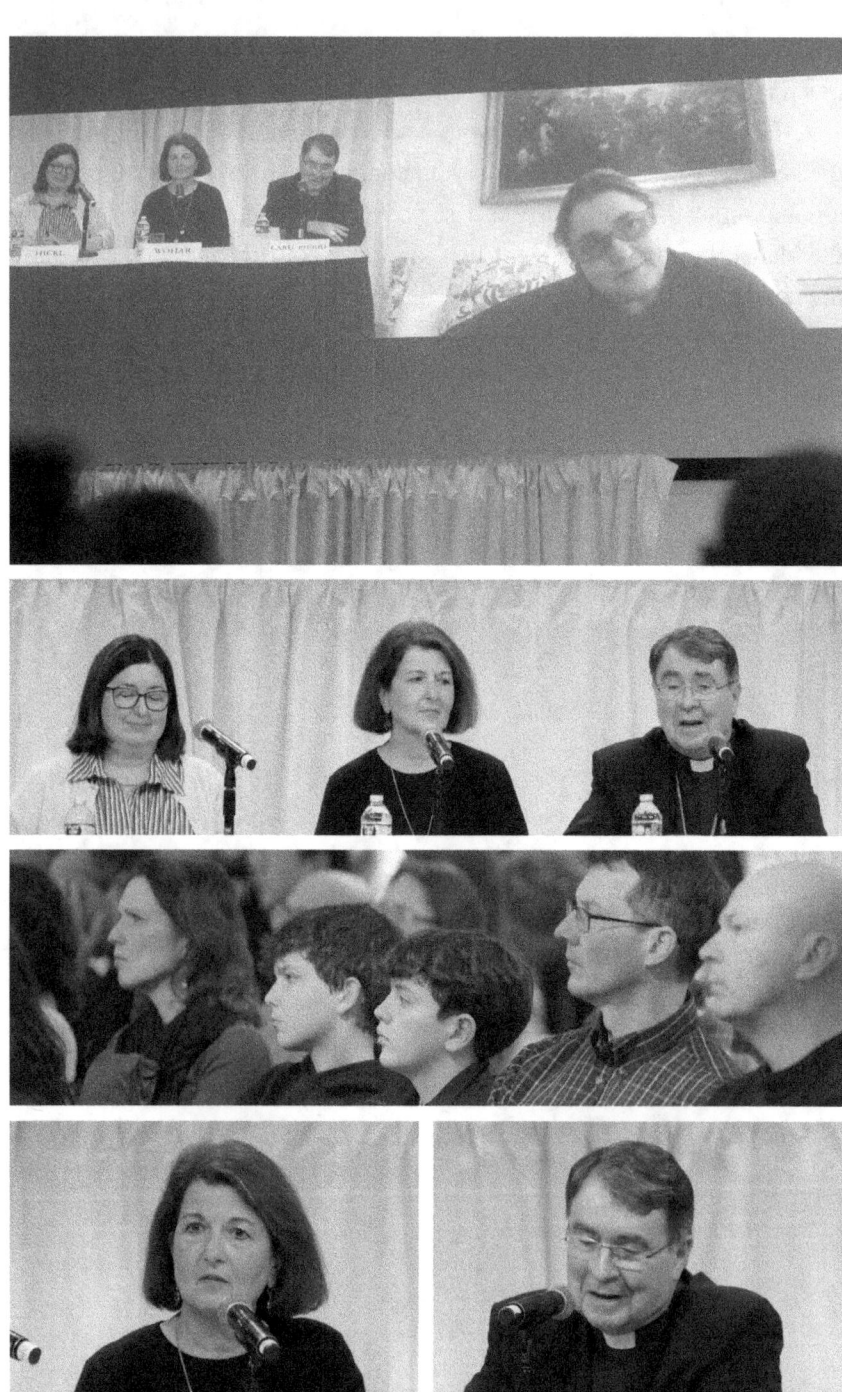

A New Life

Two young modern saints: Carlo Acutis and Pier Giorgio Frassati, presented by **Cardinal Christophe Pierre**, *Papal Nuncio to the U.S,* **Antonia Salzano**, *Carlo Acutis' mother, and* **Christine Wohar**, *Founder, FrassatiUSA, Inc. Moderated by* **Amy Hickl**, *Dean of Faculty, Notre Dame Academy School, Los Angeles.*

Introduction

"There is a certain image of holiness that represents the exceptionality of the saint with a halo. And yet, the saint is neither a role for a few nor a piece in a museum. Holiness is the very fabric of Christian life. Given the partiality of certain images, a trace of the fundamental idea remains: the saint is not a superman; he is a true man. The saint is a true man because he adheres to God and, therefore, to the ideal for which his heart was made, of which his destiny is made. Ethically, all of this means 'to do the will of God' within a humanity that remains human and yet becomes different. Saint Paul testifies to the Galatians: 'While living in the flesh, I live by faith in the Son of God.' In fact, holiness is the reflection of the only One in whom humanity was fulfilled according to all its potentiality: Jesus Christ.'"

— Fr. Luigi Giussani, *In Search of the Human Face*, Slant Books 2025

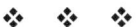

Amy Hickl, moderator: Good evening, everyone. My name is Amy Hickl. I'm the Dean of Faculty at Notre Dame Academy in Los Angeles, and I'm very happy to welcome you all here tonight, both those here at the pavilion with us and those joining us online to our final event: "A New Life." This evening, we come together at the end of our days of journeying through the encounter to reflect on two young men whose lives were forever changed by their encounter with Christ—Blessed Carlo Acutis and Blessed Pier Giorgio Frassati. Their lives remind us that holiness is not some unattainable ideal, but something real and vibrant and possible in my life today.

Father Giussani captured this idea beautifully in his latest book, which was recently translated to English and was presented earlier at the encounter, called *In Search of a Human Face*. Father Giussani says there's a certain image of holiness that represents the exceptionality of the saint with the halo, and yet the saint is neither a role for a few nor a piece in a museum. Holiness is the very fabric of Christian life. The saint is not a superman. He is a true man.

Both Carlo and Pier Giorgio will soon be canonized. Carlo's canonization will be in April of this year, and Pier Giorgio is scheduled for August. Their lives show us an example of the beauty and the adventure of living this new life.

To help us this evening explore their lives and witness, we are very fortunate to have with us tonight two special guests. Christine Wohar is here. She's the founder of Frassati USA and has dedicated her work to sharing the life and witness of Pier Giorgio Frassati. Frassati was a man of deep faith, contagious joy, and devotion to Christ. He was born in 1901 in Turin, Italy, and became known for his adventurous spirit, his love for the Eucharist, and passion for prayer. He shared his faith freely, inspiring friends to seek God in daily life. Moved by his love for Christ, he devoted himself endlessly to serving the poor, the sick, everyone around him in need. He was also an avid mountain climber, and he embodied the phrase *verso l'alto*—to the heights—both in his love for nature and in his spiritual journey towards God. He died at just 24 years old, and yet his legacy continues to inspire young people and all those seeking holiness in their own daily lives. This year, we're celebrating the 100th anniversary of his ascent to heaven.

It is also a great privilege to welcome online Miss Antonia Salzano, the mother of Carlo Acutis, a young man whose faith and love, also for the Eucharist, continues to inspire Catholics from around the world. Like many teenagers, Carlo enjoyed video games, soccer, technology, but what set him apart was his profound devotion to Christ. He used his talent with computers to create a website cataloging Eucharistic miracles, believing that "the Eucharist is my highway to heaven." Diagnosed with leukemia at just 15, he embraced his suffering with faith, offering it for the Church. Before passing away, he became a model for young people today, showing that sanctity is possible for all of us.

We're very blessed and very fortunate to be joined by his mother. To guide our conversation this evening, we're honored to have with us His Eminence, Cardinal Christophe Pierre, the Apostolic Nuncio to the United States. He's going to help us reflect more deeply on the lives of these two extraordinary young men and how their witness continues to inspire us today. So Your Eminence, I turn it over to you.

Cardinal Christophe Pierre: Yes, thank you for inviting me to have a few questions about the life of these two extraordinary gentlemen. I greet you all, and I greet Antonia, the mother of Carlo Acutis.

Actually, it's interesting to see that we are in the presence of the mother of a young man who, not so long ago, died and very shortly will be canonized by Pope Francis. Imagine—that's beautiful. It's a time of grace, you know. And I feel very happy to do that, you know, because basically the purpose of our life is holiness. But we need to have models, you know. The saints in the life of the Church—there are many, many, many. They are offered to us as a gift from God, so that we may have a kind of direction. And we have today two good examples, you know.

So I will not speak too much, because I would like to ask a few questions. We have Carlo Acutis and Pier Giorgio Frassati. Pier Giorgio was born at the beginning of the last century, so it's not so long ago. When my father and my mother were born, he was still alive. So for me, it's not too long ago, because he died, I think, in 1925—the beginning of the last century. I was not born myself.

I would like to ask—and of course, we don't have the mother of Pier Giorgio, but we have a good lady, Christine Wohar, who actually spent a good time of her life inquiring about his life and she's in love, indeed, is that correct, with the life of this man? I will have also to ask. I will leave the two guests to speak.

So I would like to have a first question. When you see these people, they were actually ordinary people like us. Not all of you are ordinary—some are extraordinary, but nobody knows! But Carlo and Pier Giorgio grew up, by the way, in well-to-do families. It's interesting. Although in different historical contexts, they all came from Italy. How did they become interested—that's interesting, that's a good point—interested in the life of Christ in their environment? Because at some stage, when you study the life of the two, you realize that their family was not necessarily interested in their own interest in Christ.

Maybe Antonia will tell us something about that. What happens in her life? It's wonderful, because I remember I received my faith from my mother and my father, and there's a kind of continuity. It's interesting to see that the son of a mother helped the mother to have an encounter with Christ. It's interesting. I'm puzzled about that.

How did they become interested in the life of Christ in their environment? Can you tell a story or two of their initial encounter with Christ and how these affected their family life? Welcome.

Antonia Salzano: Good afternoon, everybody. So Carlo... normally, the stories of the saints is that they were grown in a very Catholic and devoted family. But in the case of Carlo, it's the contrary, because I was not so good a Catholic. I was terrible, because I was raised in a family—I was an only child, and I was lucky because I was living in Rome, in the center, close to Piazza Venezia, where around there are only Catholic schools. So I was sent to a Catholic school. But my parents unfortunately never brought me to Mass because, I mean, they baptized me because it was normal in the family in Italy to baptize, but I was not at all raised in a practicing family.

So my first Holy Communion was my first communion when I did it because all the class, my classroom, they were doing the preparation for the first Holy Communion. Then the confirmation was the second Holy Communion, and then my marriage probably was the third one. I'm not exaggerating. But anyway, so in this environment, I don't know why God chose me, but you know, sometimes he uses the worst to bring out his greatness. So he chose me, who was absolutely not a special Catholic or whatever.

So I had Carlo. I got married very young with my husband—and we were in London, and Carlo was always running ahead of time. I always say this: he was very advanced with respect to the other children. Three months, the first word; five months, he started to speak. And with the faith as well, it was very advanced. And I cared very much about my parental position. I wanted to be trustworthy and also a witness for him in every aspect of life. But with the faith, I was really lacking because I didn't know anything. I was so ignorant, and Carlo was so deep with the questions he posed to me that he created in me an instability. I was, in a certain way, not at ease with his questions, because I felt that there was a lack in me of something.

Then I had the sudden death of my father, who died of a heart attack. He was very young. I was, as I said, an only child. So the problem is that it was an unexpected death. And this created in me really a sorrow, a very big sorrow, and I started questioning about what is after life, what happens, why this death? Where is my father? All the questions that you normally start to pose to yourself when you lose a very beloved person.

And three months after the death of my father, Carlo had an apparition of my father, and he asked Carlo to pray for him, because he was in Purgatory. And I am sure that it was a true mystical thing that Carlo had, because Carlo was merely five and a half years old, and since then, he was so impressed by this that he never stopped praying for the souls in Purgatory. All his life, he used to pray for them.

And these things, of course, created worries for me. But I was lucky because I met in my life... I was lucky because I had the chance to meet a very holy priest. He was very old when I met him. He was already in his old age, and he was living in Bologna. And he was called the Padre Pio of Bologna. So he was very well known for his holiness. He was a special person. And I remember that once I went to Bologna, and I met him. I called him, and he received me straight away. And when he received me, he started to tell me things about my son. He didn't know anything about me. And he started to tell me that Carlo would be very famous for the Church, very important. He had a special mission. Such great things he was saying to me that I was really astonished. I was thinking to myself, maybe he will become Pope or bishop, who knows? Because speaking this way, I didn't understand very well. But then he confessed me, and he told me all my sins—he had the discernment of the Spirit. So this was really special. Can you imagine? I was frightened at this meeting. It was terrible for me.

And since that moment, I really started with Carlo, because we can say that we had this path together, and I started to follow my son. He wanted to go to Mass, to enter the church, even if he didn't have the chance to do the first Holy Communion when he was seven years old. But I always say that Carlo was my savior, because through Carlo I understood the importance of the Eucharist. For me, before, the sacraments were only symbols. I was like a Protestant, a perfect Protestant. I didn't believe in baptism, in the Eucharist, in anything. I thought that they were symbols, rituals, nothing else.

And with Carlo, I made the discovery of my life. I understood that in the Blessed Sacrament, there is the Real Presence of God among us. And this was the discovery of my life. Really the discovery, because since that moment with Carlo, we did a path, and we started to go to Mass each day, to do Eucharistic adoration each day. And we continue—I continue. And this changed my life, because all the bad things that were inside me, because I was full of defects. I was very attached to material things. I was not so generous. I was not generous. I was not... I mean, a lot of things that were not holy. And really, the Eucharist transfigured me, and not only me, but also my mother, because my mother as well started to go to Mass. And we really experimented how important the Eucharist is in our life, how Jesus is really active and transfigures our life, when you open the door of your heart to Jesus and you start to become a Eucharistic soul. Really, Jesus does miracles, and I can witness this.

Carlo did his first Holy Communion when he was seven years old. And since then, he did Eucharistic adoration as well each day. And on that occasion, he wrote "to be always united with God"—this is my life program. So Carlo's program was not "I don't know what," but to be always united with God.

Cardinal Christophe Pierre: I would like you to continue, but I have a curiosity, and I think in the room, many are listening to you, and it's fascinating what you are telling us. Thank you for your witness. But you said Carlo was... you know, he had a kind of love for the Eucharist. How did it happen? At what moment did you say, "But you know, my son is interested in the Eucharist"? He was five years old. Who is there? Is there a moment when you realized that there's something strange? Because you are not interested yourself. So did you remember when and how it happened?

Antonia Salzano: It's not that it happened. He was constitutionally... I don't know how to explain... since he was born, I mean, since he had reason. And as I said, he was very advanced. He was very small, but he was... and probably in the school, the primary school with the nuns, I don't know why, he was constitutionally attracted. When he saw... he used to see a cross or a statue of the Virgin or a church, he wanted to enter, wanted to stay, praying. For me, it was fantasy. It was like a sort of habit, because it's devotion. And it was strange, but also in the behavior, it was very strange, because since it was... he was so generous, always very obedient. I don't remember a time in which I had to shout at Carlo, to say, "You have to do this. You have to do that." Now I have a son and a daughter. Of course, they are very good persons, but...

Cardinal Christophe Pierre: Don't tell them. Don't tell them. [*audience laughter*]

Antonia Salzano: They are 15 years old. Imagine, even if they're very good, of course. I mean, Carlo was really special, and me and my husband, just to understand how we already knew this, even if we were, you know, profane, it's the fact that I used to call him *Il mio Buddha*, because for me, Buddha was the light, and I used to call him, when he was born, because he was always smiling, so obedient, so generous, so special. And he was thinking of other people, and already me and my husband were surprised about how he was. The way he was was not normal. Just to tell you that already me and my husband called him "little little Buddha." Then, of course, growing, you know, advanced, because when he was seven years old, he didn't have the head of a seven-year-old boy. He had the head of an 11-year-old boy. So everything was advanced. So I don't know how to explain, and of course, also with the computer, all the things you know that people always talk about...

Cardinal Christophe Pierre: We'll talk about that a bit later, if you allow me. So I think what is interesting is that, suddenly, at the beginning of his life, he had been touched by Jesus, and especially, you know, a kind of attraction for the Eucharist. And he was different, you know. And you are not yourself, but so you realize that there was something in your son. I think it's unbelievable. It's very interesting.

So if you allow me, I would like to ask... Christine Wohar? Christine? I prefer Christine because I cannot pronounce Wohar. So tell us about Pier Giorgio. He's a different kind of person. He lived a little before, but also an extraordinary person. And both of them had actually an experience of the encounter with Christ inside the family, which was not necessarily... they didn't receive that from their family, but it happened.

Christine Wohar: Well, first I want to just congratulate Antonia Salzano on the canonization of her son. I can't imagine the contrast of losing your child and then seeing him raised to the altar as a saint. So I feel so privileged to be here with you, and also with you, Cardinal Pierre, and I'm so grateful to be asked to be here. And as she was speaking—I could listen to her all night—the similarity with Pier Giorgio is so striking. Carlo was born 90 years after Pier Giorgio. Pier Giorgio in 1901 and Carlo in 1991. But the similarities of their stories are just striking.

Although Mrs. Salzano has said that she followed Carlo in his spiritual life, whereas with Pier Giorgio that wasn't the case. So we often read that his parents, his father, was agnostic. They say he was not a practicing Catholic, and his mother was... I think she fulfilled the obligations of a good Catholic woman—what she would do, she had her children baptized and confirmed and so on. But Pier Giorgio didn't have the example of a family that prayed in the home together, and yet he, like I was hearing with Carlo, had some kind of inner charism, this grace, the action of the Holy Spirit, I guess.

As a small boy, without that example in the home, the stories are told of him, even at four years old, opening the door and seeing a beggar woman with a child with no shoes or socks, and he took his off immediately and gave them to her and shut the door. Pier Giorgio once heard that Jesus didn't have a father. He misunderstood about Saint Joseph, and so he was very upset and crying that Jesus was an orphan, distraught until his mother told him no, he had two fathers, a heavenly father and an earthly father, to console him, because as a little boy, this troubled him.

And in his case, he could not receive the Eucharist at age seven. That wasn't changed until later in his lifetime. So he received the Eucharist later. But this was, like Carlo, the transformative moment in his spiritual life, because because of a circumstance of failing Latin—our happy fault in the life of Pier Giorgio—he went to a Catholic school run by the Jesuit fathers, and there they encouraged him to receive the Eucharist daily at age 12. But he needed the permission of his mother, and she didn't want to give permission, not because she had any opposition to the Eucharist, but she thought it would become common, a habit, and it was very rare at those times.

And so the most famous story about Pier Giorgio with the Eucharist is that he came into the headmaster one day, knocked on the door and in Italian, he said, "*Ho vinto! Ho vinto!*" I won! I won! And the headmaster said, "You won the lottery, Pier Giorgio?" He was teasing him. And Pier Giorgio said, "I won permission from my mother to receive communion every day." Now, 12 years old. At 12 years old, that wasn't the most important thing in my life. At 12 years old, he kept that appointment, they say. We say that he never missed going to the Eucharist daily until his death, unless something very dramatic happened.

In Pier Giorgio's case, however, unlike Carlo, his family didn't follow this. They didn't understand him, and so he had to do things in a creative way, such as he had this system that he used when he wanted to go to morning Mass in the summer home. And he would tie a rope to himself and hang it out of the window, and the gardener would come and pull the rope and tug it so he could wake up without waking up his family and run outside and go up to church early. So it wasn't that his family didn't come along with him. In fact, they really never understood him, even at the time of his death, his great devotion to the Eucharist. But like in Carlo's case, that was the transformative moment, I think, that special encounter with the Eucharist, as it is, I guess, with all of the saints.

Cardinal Christophe Pierre: It's interesting that for the two boys, they belong to a family who has not given them the experience with the Lord, but the Lord is taking the initiative. It's interesting. But on the other side, you see the presence of the Church with these two boys, and particularly through the Eucharist.

In some way, in spite of the ignorance, in spite of even the resistance from the environment, the Eucharist went to them. I think it's so important today. We, the bishops in this country, three years ago, decided to have a kind of Eucharistic revival, Eucharistic renewal, to help precisely ourselves. The Christians not to forget the power of the Eucharist, even in environment... The bishops noted that many people, even Catholics, do not believe in the real presence of Christ in the Eucharist. And what has happened? Even ourselves, at times, we don't believe it. Even ourselves, we forget what the Eucharist is. We don't give the importance to the Eucharist. And you see these two young boys, surprised their fathers and their mothers. It's beautiful.

So I would like to ask another question. Both Carlo and Pier Giorgio had an intense and rich life. They were extraordinary persons. I think it's good. I think the saint is a real human being, not isolated from humanity. On the contrary, and they were full of friends. Can you tell us about their friendships? Carlo at school, Pier Giorgio with his friends. And, you know, he had a lot of initiatives. I read somewhere that they had... he had a kind of association with, they call it in Italian, *tipitoski*–a kind of band of friends, whatever it was. So Antonia, tell us about the friendships of your son.

Antonia Salzano: Carlo, basically, was very nice, very joyful. He had a lot of friends. He had a normal life, as you say, but he was not an alien, luckily. And it was a normal... but normality... our normality, because everybody, we are all human beings. But if we open the door of our heart to God, our normality becomes always extraordinary. It is really... the life of Carlo shows that normality in Christ becomes extraordinary, because Carlo used to live with the presence of God inside him, and he was a witness because he lived everything. He used to do everything in Jesus, for Jesus, and through Jesus, and he used to say that we are all mystics because we received the baptism. The Holy Trinity is inside us. But what is important is to connect with His presence in the daily life, not only when I go to Mass,

I go to the meeting, or sometimes as a moment of prayer. All the day has to be a connection with God.

And Carlo really felt that. Carlo had this connection. He felt that God was the first friend of Carlo. And when you live this relationship with God, you trust... it's like if you were contagious of Christ. You contagious everybody. So we are not... he didn't have this special duty to be... to have a special relationship with his friends. They felt they were attracted. Some of them were not believers. Some of them were attracted because of the quality of Carlo, like loyalty, like generosity, like the way he used to help friends when they had difficulties in the schools, homework, with the computer. He used to... he started to teach catechesis when he was 11 years old. First he was helping catechesis, and then he became a catechist, and this is the reason why he did his Eucharistic miracle exhibition that is going all over the world. He did it because he realized that people don't understand the importance of the Eucharist.

And with his friends, it was... it was easy. When he died, in his classroom, even if... just to tell you which type of classroom he had: he was studying at the Jesuit school, and once there was a debate about abortion, and Carlo was the only one that was contrary to abortion. All the other his friends were pro-abortion, and Carlo was the only one who was against. But nevertheless, I mean, even if Carlo had different ideas from his classmates, everybody, when he died, all the classroom had a sort of depression, and they started to say, "What will we do without Carlo?" It was like if somebody vital for them had died.

And so this is just to tell you how he had this charisma of getting well with everybody. He was very generous to help people, especially the bullied people, the young people that were bullies. Since he was the first... the first class, the primary school, he was always defending bullied people, or the people or young people with handicaps, and all the professors that he had during the school life, they were all witnesses of this behavior of Carlo. He was being like a father figure to help, especially the shy young people who had difficulties to get on with the other classmates. I mean, the way he was always going towards these people, they became the best friends. And this was really incredible, because since he was six years old, he was always like this.

And of course, what can I say about Carlo? Unfortunately, even if he studied in Catholic school, most of his classmates were not believers, not practicing. So for Carlo, it was also a difficulty, because he couldn't show completely what he was inside, because... but Carlo understood that he couldn't be forcing this. He knew when he could speak, when he could not speak, when he could witness. But firstly, with these people, he witnessed with his loyalty, his generosity, his smile, always being at the disposal of everybody. So this was a characteristic of "Buddha."

And of course, it's difficult to live in an environment like this. Milano is a very difficult town, because even if we are in Italy, Milano is very much projected on business. So people are very distracted, very taken from the money, the success, the power, and also the young boys that are in these schools, especially the schools that are in the center of Milano, where we used to live, unfortunately they are very taken by all these ideas, which are not Christ and not the Gospel, but different ideas. And unfortunately, this was really difficult to handle for Carlo, but nevertheless, everybody was in love with Carlo in the real sense. Everybody.

When he died, at the funeral, the church was so full that a lot of people had to remain outside the church. And among these people, there were beggars, there were people of other nationalities, because Carlo really had... he was like... he used to bring sleeping bags to give to beggars we had around our house, because unfortunately, as I said, we were living in the center of Milano. Like New York. Unfortunately, there are a lot... I was three times recently... I saw a lot in the street recently.

Cardinal Christophe Pierre: It's not a small town in New York, and... So, what is interesting in what you say, Antonia, is that Carlo was a real human being, and with a great quality of relationship, and a great sense of sensitivity, the capacity to relate. He was not a strange person. I think it's also one characteristic. So I would like to ask you, Christine, how was Pier Giorgio in his relationships, his friendships, his family? Because he was not a loner.

Christine Wohar: Pier Giorgio was, as they said, an explosion of joy, an explosion of joy. And I think his friendships took on an extra importance because his home life wasn't very happy. His parents did not have a good marriage, and they were, in fact, on the verge of a legal separation at the time of his death, which would have been very shameful, not a good thing for a family at that time, and so it was not pleasant in the home. And his friends really were his outlet.

And you mentioned that he formed this group he called the *tipitoski*, which never really translates well in English, like "the sinister ones" or "the shady characters" or whatever. And people sometimes will write me, and they want to know what were all of the rules of that organization. They want to start one. And his rules were, he said, "Siamo pochi ma buoni come maccheroni." "We're few, but good, like macaroni"–that was the motto. I mean, it was a joke, really. It was... he was a big practical joker. But his real reason for that group was his friends were starting to get married and finish school and move away, and he wanted a way to keep them together. And so he said, "I would like for us to pledge a pact that has no earthly limits or temporal boundaries: union and prayer."

And so when he did anything with his friends, he was always trying to do things to lead them to Christ. So sometimes he would organize a trip to the mountains, and he would arrange for a priest to meet them at some point without them knowing, and then act surprised and say, "Oh, there's Father! We can all go to confession," you know, pray the rosary and do things, but it was always very gentle. I have in my book the story of how he would play pool with his friends–billiards–and he would make a bet that if they won, he paid them cash or something, but if he won, they had to pray the rosary or go to Mass or do something like adoration. So he was always trying to lead his friends in a gentle way.

Pier Giorgio believed that the apostolate of persuasion was the most beautiful. And they said that he made religion look attractive by the way he lived it. And nobody ever laughed at Pier Giorgio. You know, the theme of this encounter was Dante Alighieri, and Pier Giorgio was known for crazy things like just being out in the sequoia tree in the family home, reciting Dante loud enough for the neighbors to hear him, but his friends knew how he was and the deep love that he had for them.

And when he died, as she said of Carlo, thousands of people came out into the streets who had been touched by him, not just that intimate group of friends or his friends from the university, but every person he met was a friend. Every poor person that he visited anonymously felt that he was a friend. He went to the meetings of the workers who were underprivileged, and they felt like he was their friend. So Pier Giorgio said, "After parents and sisters, one of the most beautiful affections is that of friendship," and that really defined the way he lived his life outside of the home.

Cardinal Christophe Pierre: So, you know, that's one of the very important aspects. We realize in these two young men there is a kind of special relationship with Christ, the Eucharist, but also very interesting, normal relationships with friends, with a lot of people. So it tells us a lot for today about what holiness is.

There is something which maybe it would be interesting... I don't know if the mother of Carlo could tell us, you know, how was... you will tell us also, in your research, how was the prayer of Carlo, how was the prayer of Pier Giorgio? We know that they were... they had a special attraction to the Eucharist. But the Eucharist is the presence of Christ. What was the personal relationship with Christ? Have you, as a mother, have you experienced that yourself? Antonia?

Antonia Salzano: Definitely, because daily meeting with Jesus in the Eucharist, in the Blessed Sacrament. He used to do Eucharistic adoration each day. So he used to speak with Jesus, like with a friend. He had really a mystical life that continues in his... continues this meeting with Jesus that was the center of his life. Consider that when we used to do a trip abroad, the first worry of Carlo was to look for the nearest church to our hotel, not to lose the Mass, or not to lose the encounter with Jesus. So Carlo was really centered in Christ. For him, it was everything. All the day was going around the appointment with Jesus in the Blessed Sacrament.

Of course, this continues... this meeting. Then he brings in his life, in his daily life, Christ donates himself to us from the Eucharist, and in that school of Jesus, Carlo learned how to donate himself to the others, so all the charity works he used to do. But the characteristic of Carlo was this special union with Jesus, as I said before. The fact... everything he used to do, he used to do in Jesus, through Jesus and with Jesus. So he used to also donate some little moments to Jesus to do a prayer, to read the Bible... to do the *Liturgy delle Ore* [Liturgy of the Hours], to pray the rosary, that was a daily prayer also, because Carlo used to say that the rosary was the most important prayer of his life, and he had a special, really special devotion to the Virgin Mary. But he used to have continuously this relation with Jesus. He never stopped. I felt this. This was very particular, probably the Carthusian monks and the cloistered monks and nuns have this sort of relation. And it was very particular how Carlo could bring this interiority in the daily things of his life, in the sports, with the friends, and also in our house, you felt this.

And he used to say that everybody should be like him, because we have God inside us, and if we do everything for Jesus and we offer our life, it becomes a continuous prayer. So this is the secret—the secret of transforming our love in a continuous prayer—is what Carlo did. And it's possible. This is possible, but we need the force of our will, because we have to ask Jesus to grow in this intimacy with him. And of course, the Eucharist is the highway for this intimacy. Why? Jesus himself in the Gospel of Saint John, Chapter Six says, "People who eat my flesh and drink my blood remain in me, and I will remain in them." So we know that through the Eucharist, we create a special union, and this union has to continue, not only in the Mass when we do the adoration, but in the daily life, in all the steps of our life.

And what is the moment... or as Carlo used to say, to see how God has the first place in our life is to see during the day, how many times do I turn to God? Do I pray to God? Do I have recourse to God? Do I thank God for all what he's given me? How many times? And if we start to do first, maybe, it's a short space, you know, and then little by little, if we will try to grow in this space, we will see how our life will become completely in God and will be transfigured. And we will live, as Carlo used to say, in the co-eternity of God. We will already be in the infinite life, and we have the peace. We really experiment this.

Cardinal Christophe Pierre: What is interesting in this beautiful... it's interesting to see a little child who had the prayer life as a relationship with Christ, with Jesus. I think it's important. I remember... I think all of us have been in some way educated in the faith by our parents. But I remember the first prayers I had. They were from my mother, my father. And we are speaking to Jesus. At times we have forgotten that Jesus is real, and we have to... and the mothers particularly have to present the person of Jesus. But in a way, it's wonderful to see, listening to you Antonia, that your son had this personal relationship. So thank you for that. Maybe tell us a little bit... because I'm told that we are still late, but we are never late. So I could say this.

Christine Wohar: The same things that she says. It's fascinating to hear. For Pier Giorgio, his spiritual life, of course, began with the Eucharist in the morning. He prayed the rosary. He was devoted to the Blessed Mother. He carried the rosary with him. He called it his last will and testament. He always had it with him. Once, a friend saw him carrying his rosary and said, "Oh, Pier Giorgio, you've become a religious fanatic." And he said, "No, no, I have remained a Christian. I haven't become anything, and I just remained a Christian."

He prayed the Little Office of the Blessed Virgin Mary. He would pray on the tram. He said, "You always have time to pray." He also, like Carlo, was very devoted to Eucharistic Adoration. He would go to the mountains for a skiing trip, but he would stop into the church and ask the priest to let him come in. So he said he could go to the mountains doubly strong, because he would spend that time in adoration. So very deep spiritual life, prayer life.

And one of the things that he learned in the family was from his grandmother, who taught him to remember to pray for the souls in Purgatory, as Antonia was saying earlier. And so that was another thing that was very important to Pier Giorgio. So a continuous prayer life throughout his day. His father sometimes would catch him falling asleep, kneeling at his bed, praying the rosary. And he went to the priest and said, "You need to tell my son to not do this." He said, "Would you rather he be reading some romance novel?" And if you read Pier Giorgio's letters, he quotes... reading a romance novel. So but his prayer life was very rich and full.

Cardinal Christophe Pierre: I think there is something which is amazing. Precisely, Pier Giorgio, inside his family... I think the father and the mother, as you told us, were not necessarily very much interested in religion. They were a bit puzzled by their son. They don't know what's going on. And especially the father was a senator. He was a journalist. He was a very well-known person in Italy. I think the director of *La Stampa*, right? So he saw his son as his successor. And he said, "Well, this boy is not interested in that. It's a bit strange." But what is interesting? He was never strange. He was different. And I think about what he was from the world, but he was not of the world. That's the difference. I think it tells us a lot.

So as the time has gone... I leave you to ask a few questions. Because you told me that you want to ask a few questions. I don't know.

Amy Hickl: Well, we would love, in just a couple of words, to hear from you, Antonia, and from you, Christine, what Carlo and Pier Giorgio mean to you in your life today.

Antonia Salzano: But surely, what Carlo reminds us is that there is an eternal life, that we are pilgrims of the Absolute, not of this world, and we have to live with this tension toward the absolute. And Carlo had this. When I used to ask Carlo, "What would you like to do when you're grown, when you'll be older?" or people used to ask him, he always was answering, "Who knows how long we will live? Let's be worried about the present moment. We don't know how long we will live."

He was aware about the fact that time is a creature of God. He creates time. And Jesus showed us in the 33 years he lived on the earth how to maximize life for eternity. And Carlo was aware about the importance of time, that we don't have to waste time in things that don't please God, and that God has to be our priority.

So what I think is that Carlo knew that the Eucharist is really the most powerful thing we have, the most supernatural thing we have here on the earth, because he's God among us with his real presence. As Pope Benedict used to say, with his physical presence. God is everywhere spiritually, but in the Blessed Sacrament, he's really present. And why? Because he didn't forget we are human. We have flesh and we have spirit. And he wanted to help to nourish not only our soul with the Eucharist, but also our flesh. Why? Because we have the wounds of the original sin and a lack of the will.

And Jesus through the Eucharist helps us to reinforce our force of the will, which is the way why we will become saints.

Because to become saints, for the Church, we need to live heroically virtuous. There are more than 200, but the most important are seven: faith, hope, charity, prudence, justice, fortitude, temperance, and the force of the will. And the problem is that to live regularly... we know that means not to do any more venial sin. And is it possible? Is it possible to achieve this goal? Carlo showed us that it's possible, nevertheless, the video games, internet, all the dangers we have surrounding us—the pornography, the alcohol, the drugs, the media brainwashing continuously. Nevertheless, it's possible to achieve sanctity, the goal of sanctity. And Pier Giorgio as well. He used to say, "Vivere e non vivacchiare." This is a famous... I don't know how to translate. Maybe you can translate the word *vivacchiare*. What does it... how do you translate in English? Exactly?

Christine Wohar: To live, he said, and not exist. To live and not exist.

Cardinal Christophe Pierre: You have to take life seriously.

Antonia Salzano: Not to live like... this life... I get bored. How can you get bored?

Christine Wohar: Well, I feel like I'm echoing her and copying all her answers on the test. But when Pier Giorgio was beatified in 1990 by Pope John Paul II, he said in the beatification homily, "Pier Giorgio testifies that holiness is possible for everyone." So for me, I'm sitting here today. I'm very mindful of the fact that I'm sitting here today because of the choices that this young man made 100-plus years ago, when he got up every morning and did the things he did, when he went out and served the poor, all of the sacrifices that he made. Sometimes I think, "Giorgio, you're controlling me." But it was the effect of the Body of Christ, how it shows that his choices, 100 years ago plus, are driving the things that I'm doing today. And with his canonization coming, these two saints. How wonderful that we have these two incredible lay examples for the Church this year.

Cardinal Christophe Pierre: Pier Giorgio will be canonized on August 3 and Carlo on April 27. So we are close to that. As at the beginning of this presentation, we said, I think they are a wonderful example, especially for the young people today. I see two aspects in their life: extraordinary humanity. They are people of today. They are not strange people. We can identify with them. That's wonderful. They are our brothers, and they show us the way. To be a saint is to be fully human. That's very important. The second one is their relationship with God. It's wonderful. Each one in his own way. And the third aspect, which is related, of course: they belong to the Church. They really belong to the Church. And they are people of the Eucharist. And the fourth dimension, which amazes me, is their life—they were missionaries, missionaries to the family.

Carlo has been a missionary to his mother. Antonia, you have been transformed. And thank you, Antonia. Thank you to give us your son. God bless you. Yes.

Amy Hickl: So it really is a new life. So we thank His Eminence for helping us, Christine and Antonia for their witnesses. Thank you.

Riro Maniscalco: In music, in the panorama of nature, in dreams at night, it is something else that man pays homage to, from which he expects something. He awaits it. His enthusiasm is for something that music or everything that is beautiful in the world has awakened within him. When a person begins to feel this, his soul immediately begins to await the other thing. Even in the presence of what he can grasp, he awaits another thing. He grasps what he can grasp, but he awaits another thing.

We close the encounter with the full house, and we're very grateful for that full house, which is not just a promise, it's a fact. Here begins a new life to be brought into this world, lived and shared. Thank you to the volunteers, first and foremost, and then to each and every one of us. Thank you.

New York Encounter
4 West 43rd Street
Room 611
New York, NY 10036

www.ingramcontent.com/pod-product-compliance
Lightning Source LLC
Chambersburg PA
CBHW071259220526
45468CB00001B/190